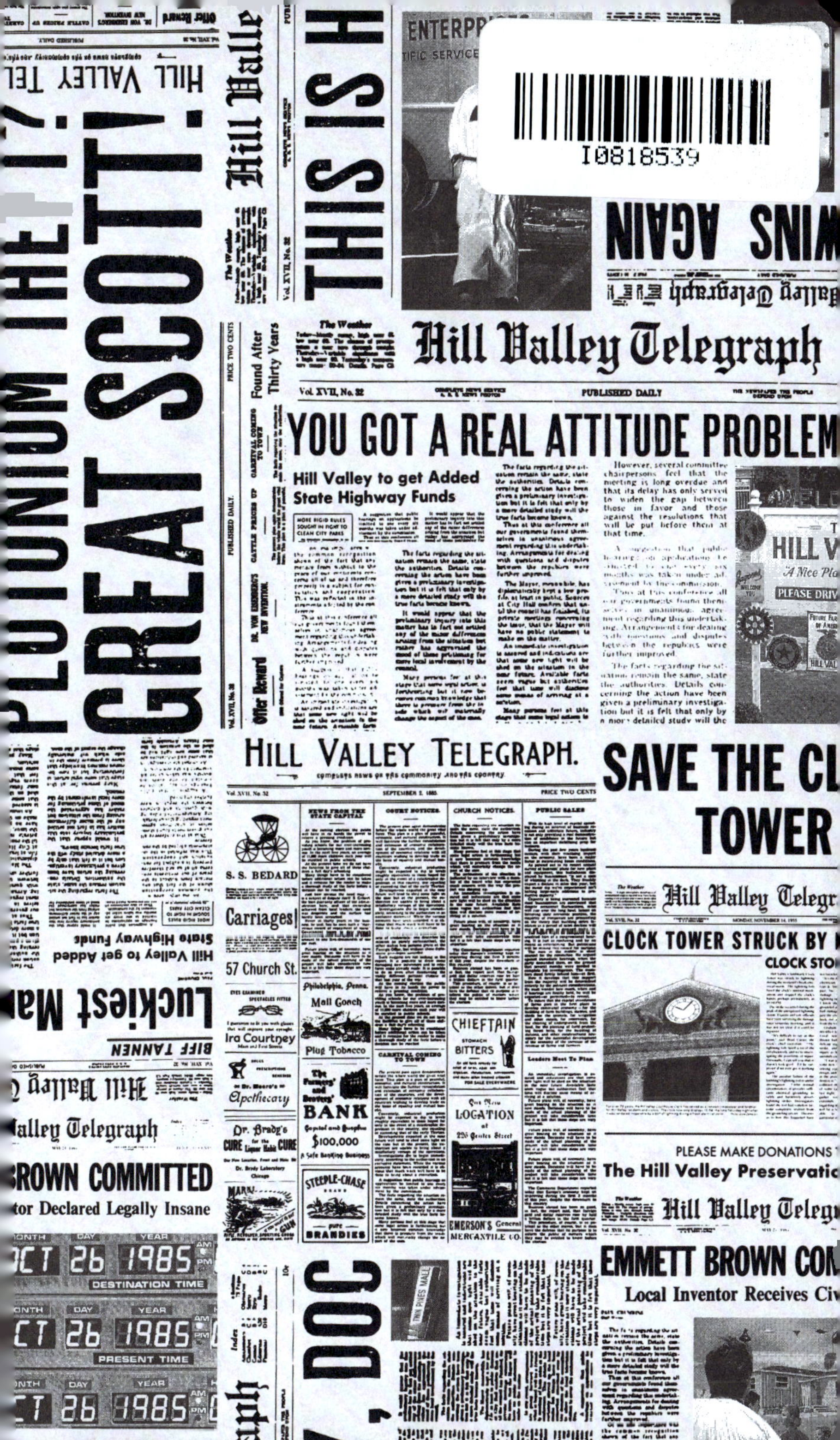

I0818539
WINS AGAIN
Hill Valley Telegraph
Vol. XVII, No. 32
PUBLISHED DAILY
YOU GOT A REAL ATTITUDE PROBLEM
Hill Valley to get Added State Highway Funds
HILL VALLEY TELEGRAPH.
SAVE THE CL
TOWER
Hill Valley Telegr
CLOCK TOWER STRUCK BY
S. S. BEDARD
Carriages
57 Church St.
CHIEFTAIN
BITTERS
BANK
$100,000
Apothecary
BRANDIES
EMERSON'S General MERCANTILE CO.
PLEASE MAKE DONATIONS
The Hill Valley Preservatic
Hill Valley Telegr
EMMETT BROWN COM
Local Inventor Receives Civ
Valley Telegraph
BROWN COMMITTED
tor Declared Legally Insane
OCT 26 1985
DESTINATION TIME
CT 26 1985
PRESENT TIME
CT 26 1985
GREAT SCOTT!
PLUTONIUM THEFT
THIS IS H
DOC

BACK TO THE FUTURE

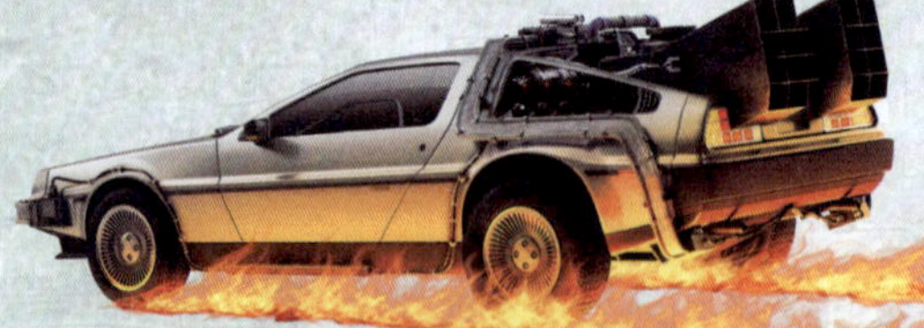

THIS BELONGS TO

CALIFORNIA
OUTATIME

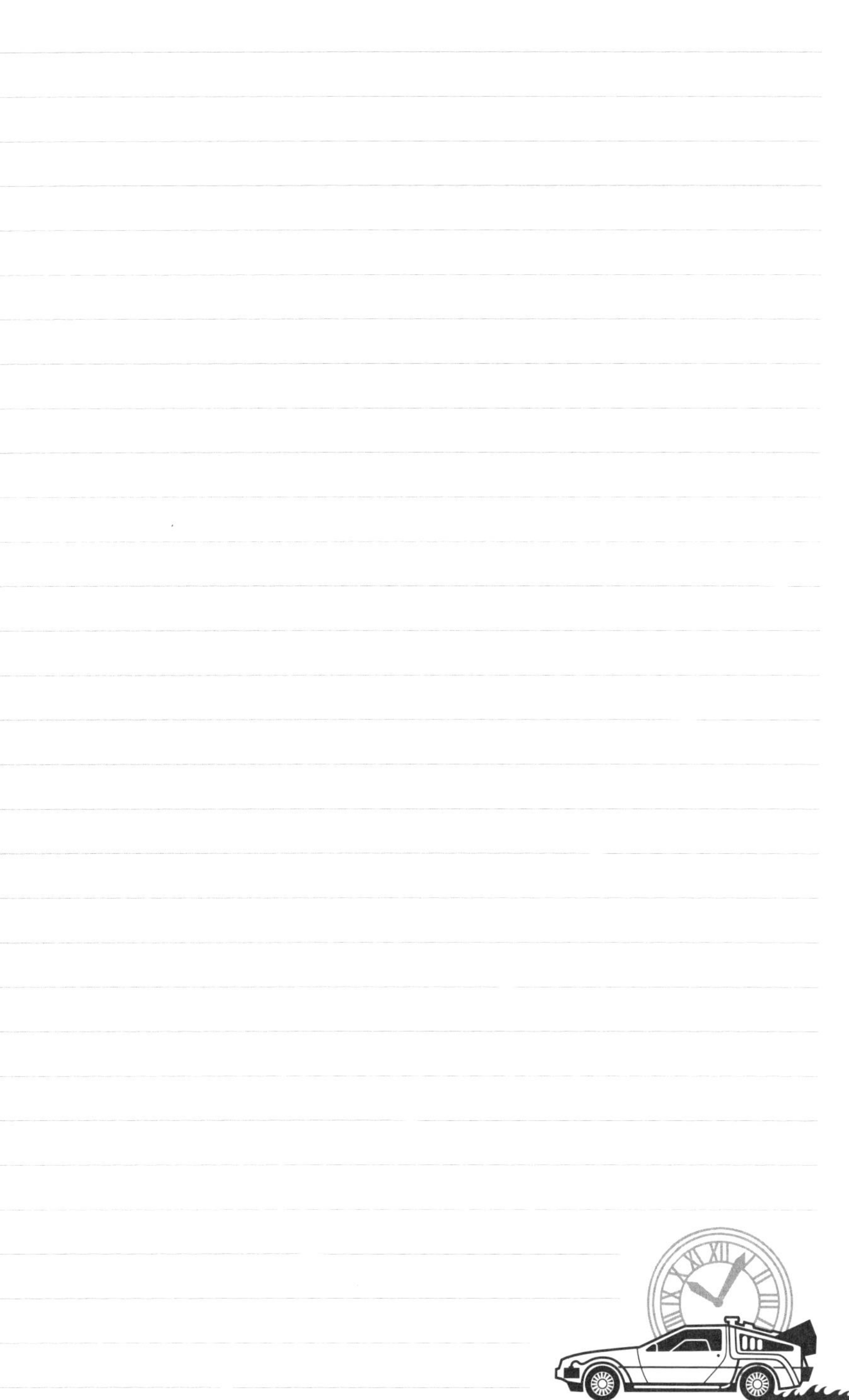

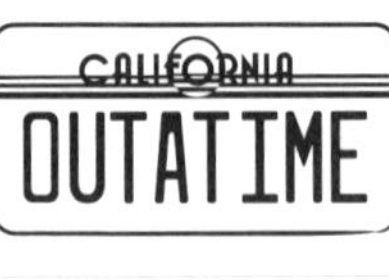
CALIFORNIA
OUTATIME

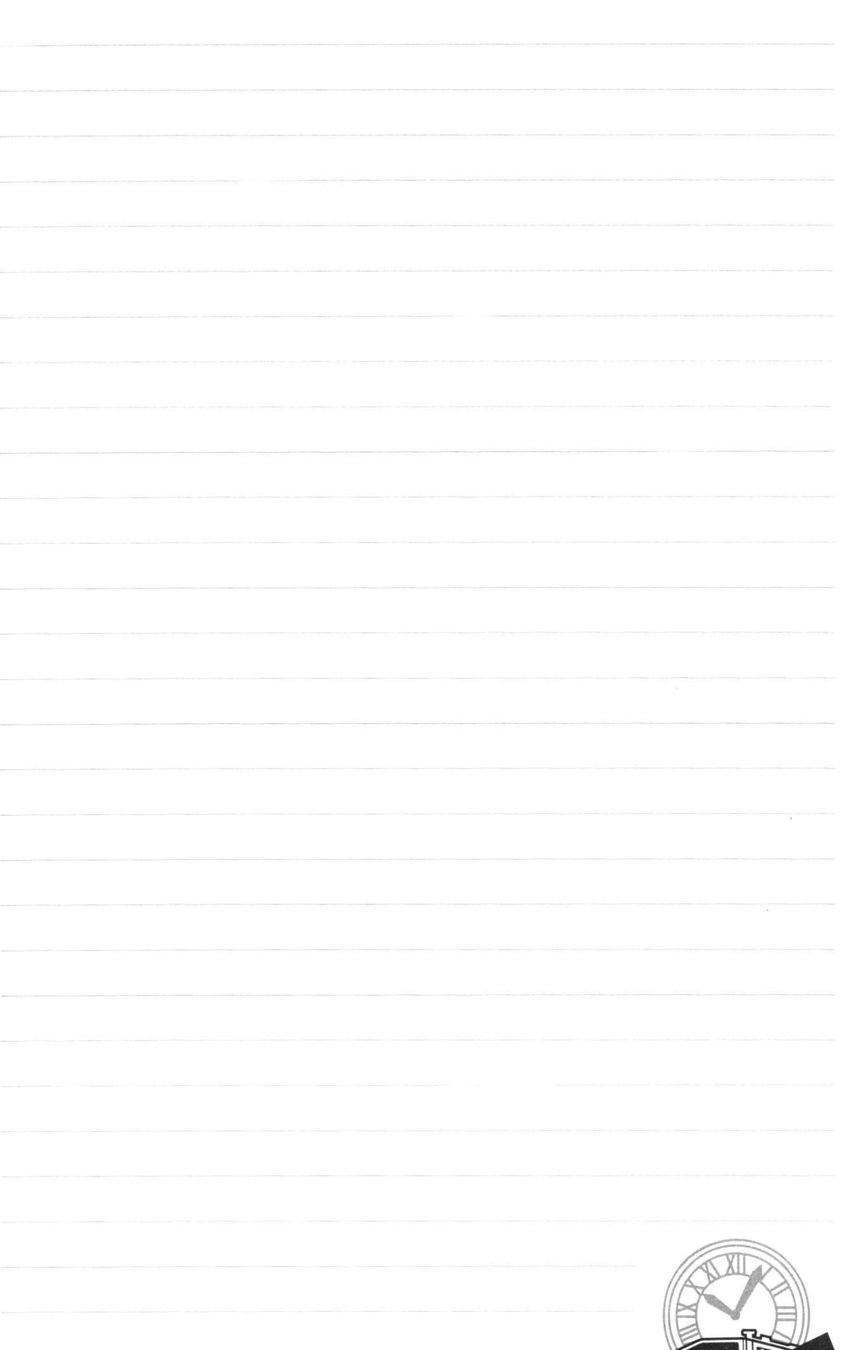

CALIFORNIA
OUTATIME

CALIFORNIA
OUTATIME

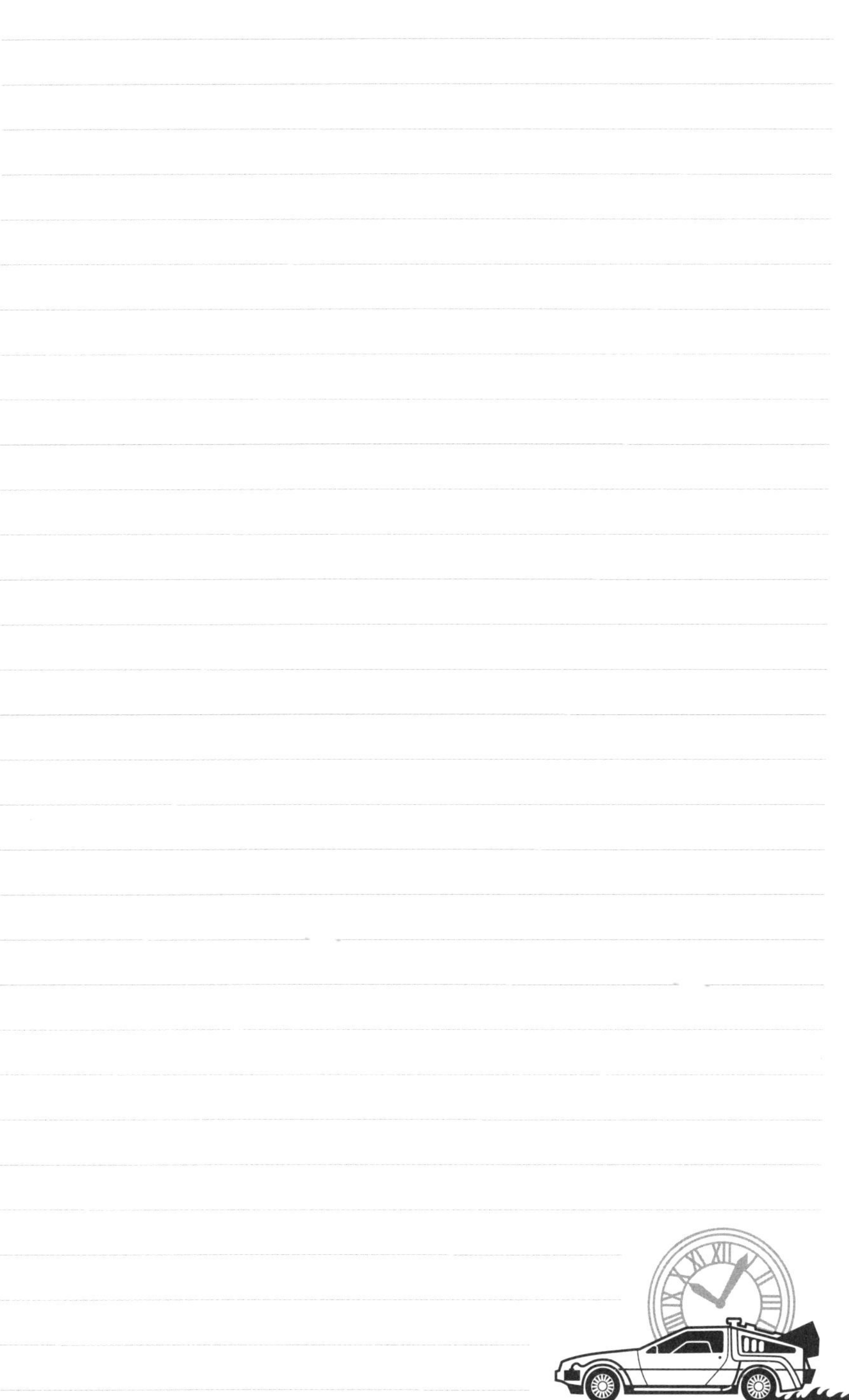

CALIFORNIA
OUTATIME

CALIFORNIA
OUTATIME

CALIFORNIA
OUTATIME

CALIFORNIA
OUTATIME

CALIFORNIA
OUTATIME

CALIFORNIA
OUTATIME

CALIFORNIA
OUTATIME

CALIFORNIA
OUTATIME

CALIFORNIA
OUTATIME

CALIFORNIA
OUTATIME

CALIFORNIA
OUTATIME

CALIFORNIA
OUTATIME

CALIFORNIA
OUTATIME

CALIFORNIA
OUTATIME

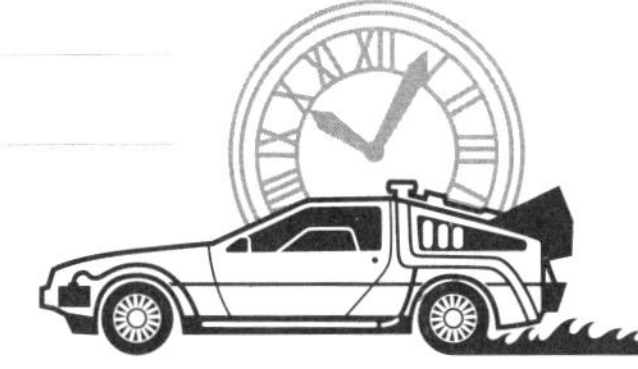

CALIFORNIA
OUTATIME

CALIFORNIA
OUTATIME

CALIFORNIA
OUTATIME

CALIFORNIA
OUTATIME

CALIFORNIA
OUTATIME

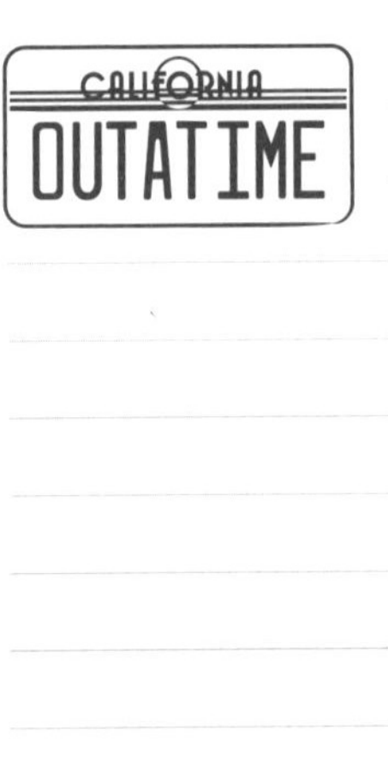
CALIFORNIA
OUTATIME

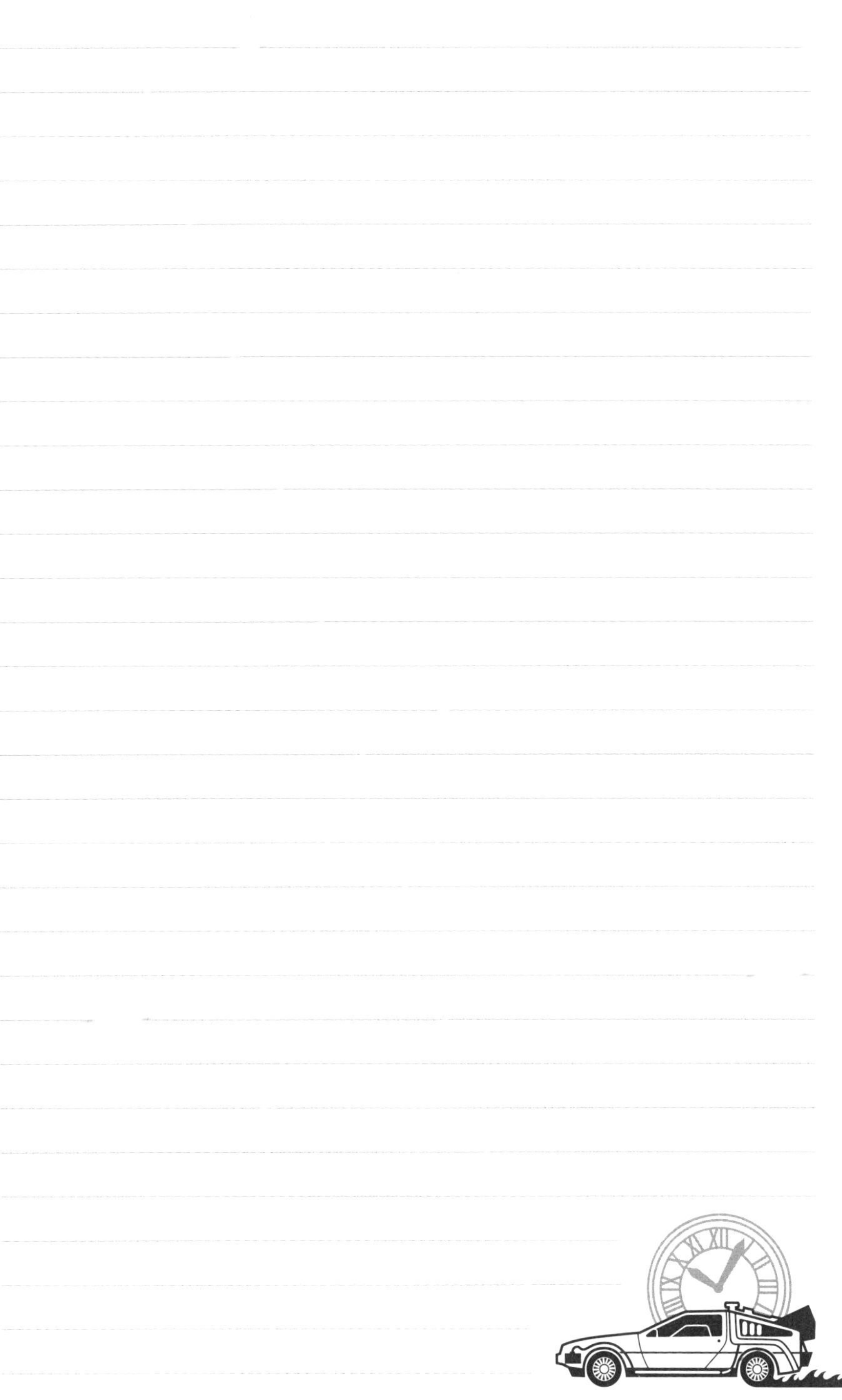

CALIFORNIA
OUTATIME

CALIFORNIA
OUTATIME

CALIFORNIA
OUTATIME

CALIFORNIA
OUTATIME

CALIFORNIA
OUTATIME

CALIFORNIA
OUTATIME

CALIFORNIA
OUTATIME

CALIFORNIA
OUTATIME

CALIFORNIA
OUTATIME

CALIFORNIA
OUTATIME

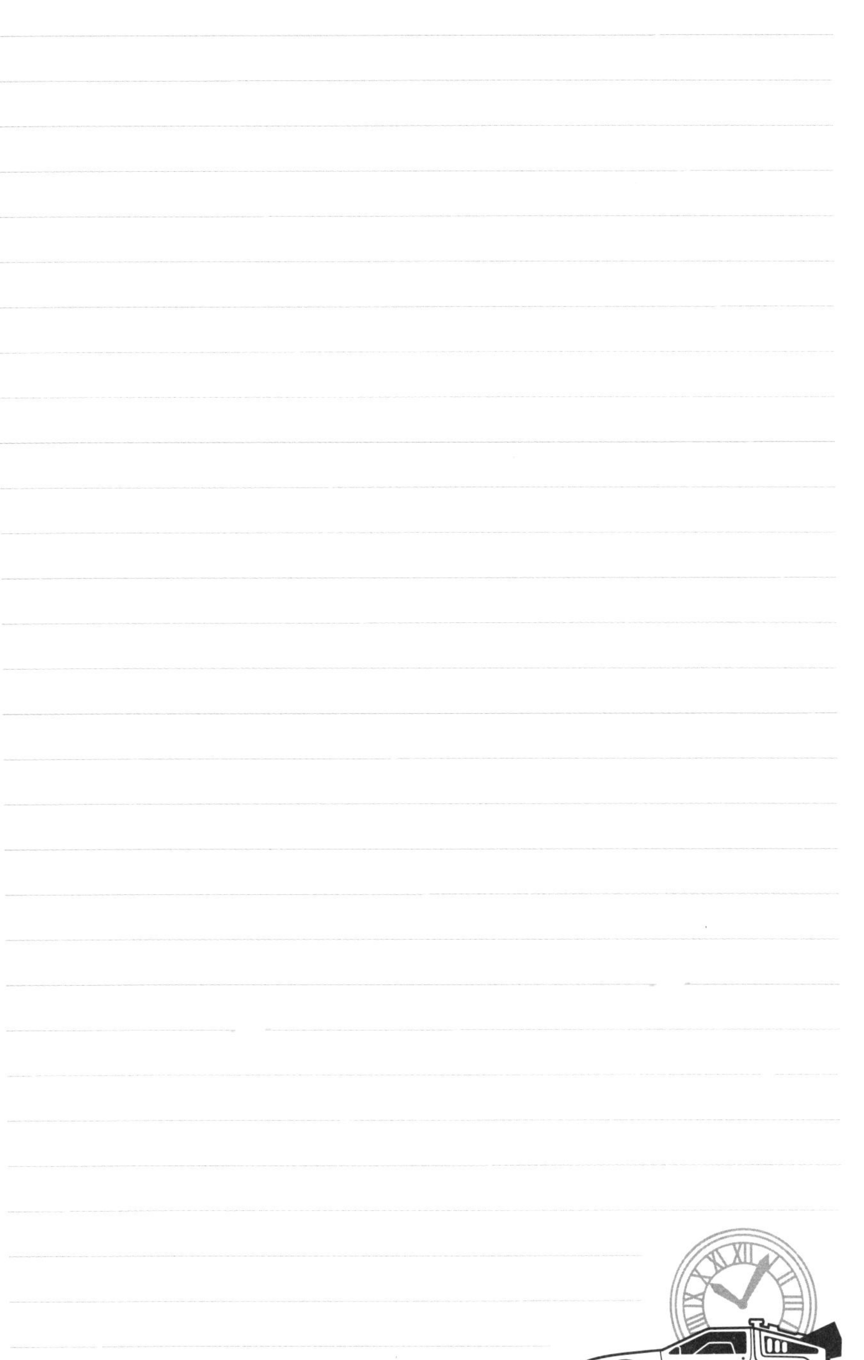

CALIFORNIA
OUTATIME

CALIFORNIA
OUTATIME

CALIFORNIA
OUTATIME

CALIFORNIA
OUTATIME

CALIFORNIA
OUTATIME

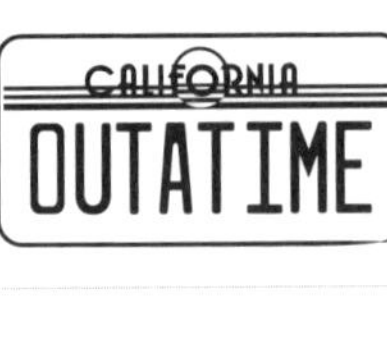
CALIFORNIA
OUTATIME

CALIFORNIA
OUTATIME

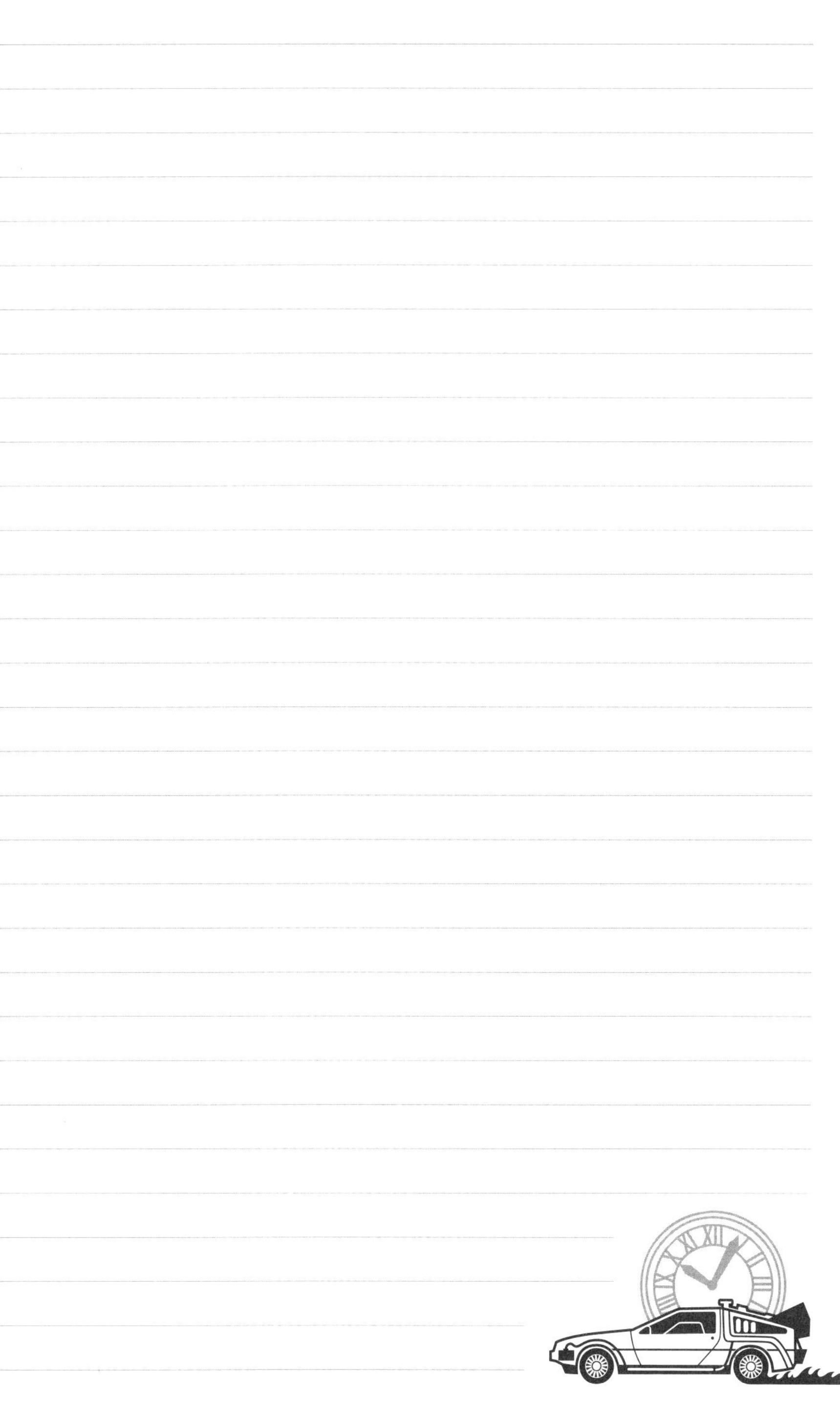

CALIFORNIA
OUTATIME

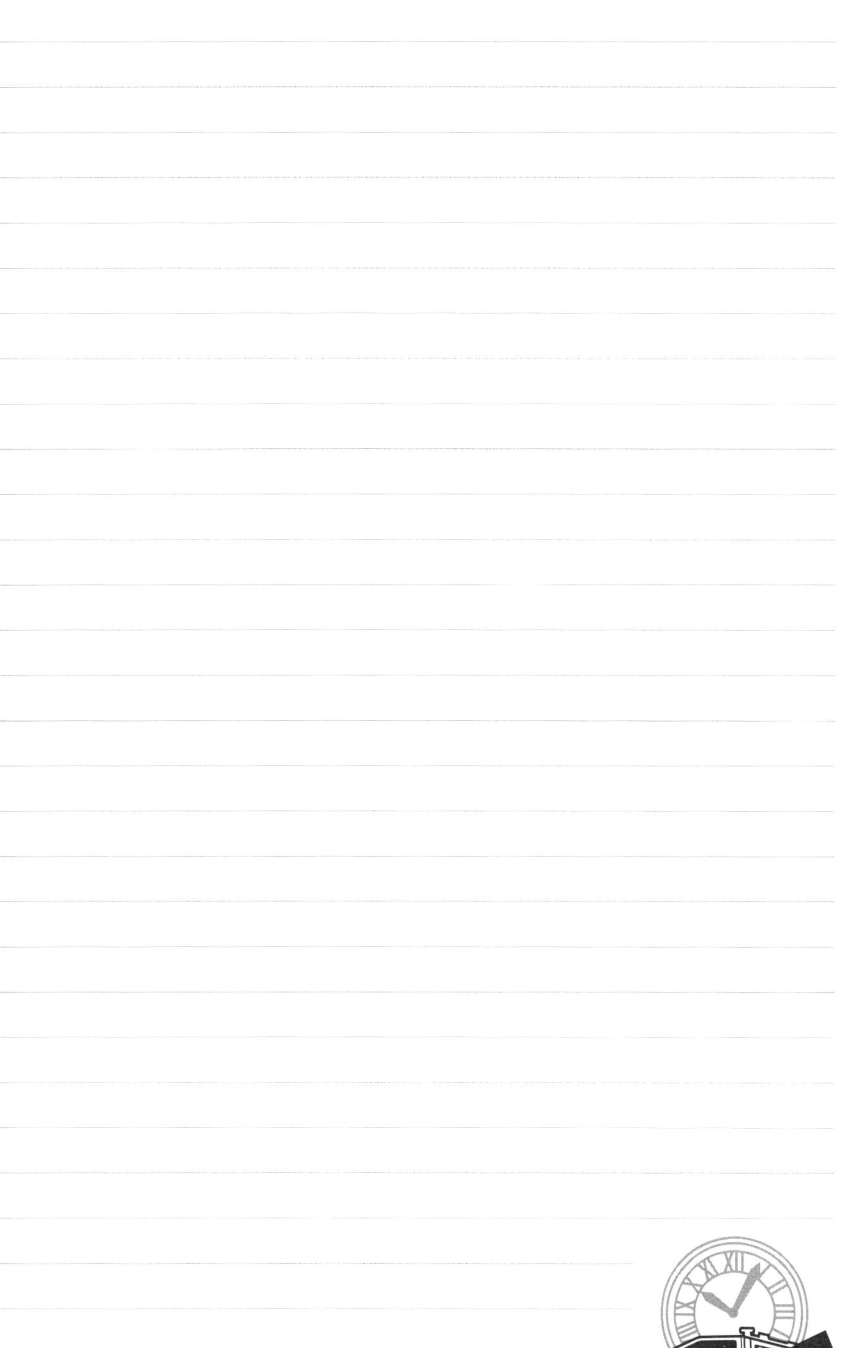

CALIFORNIA
OUTATIME

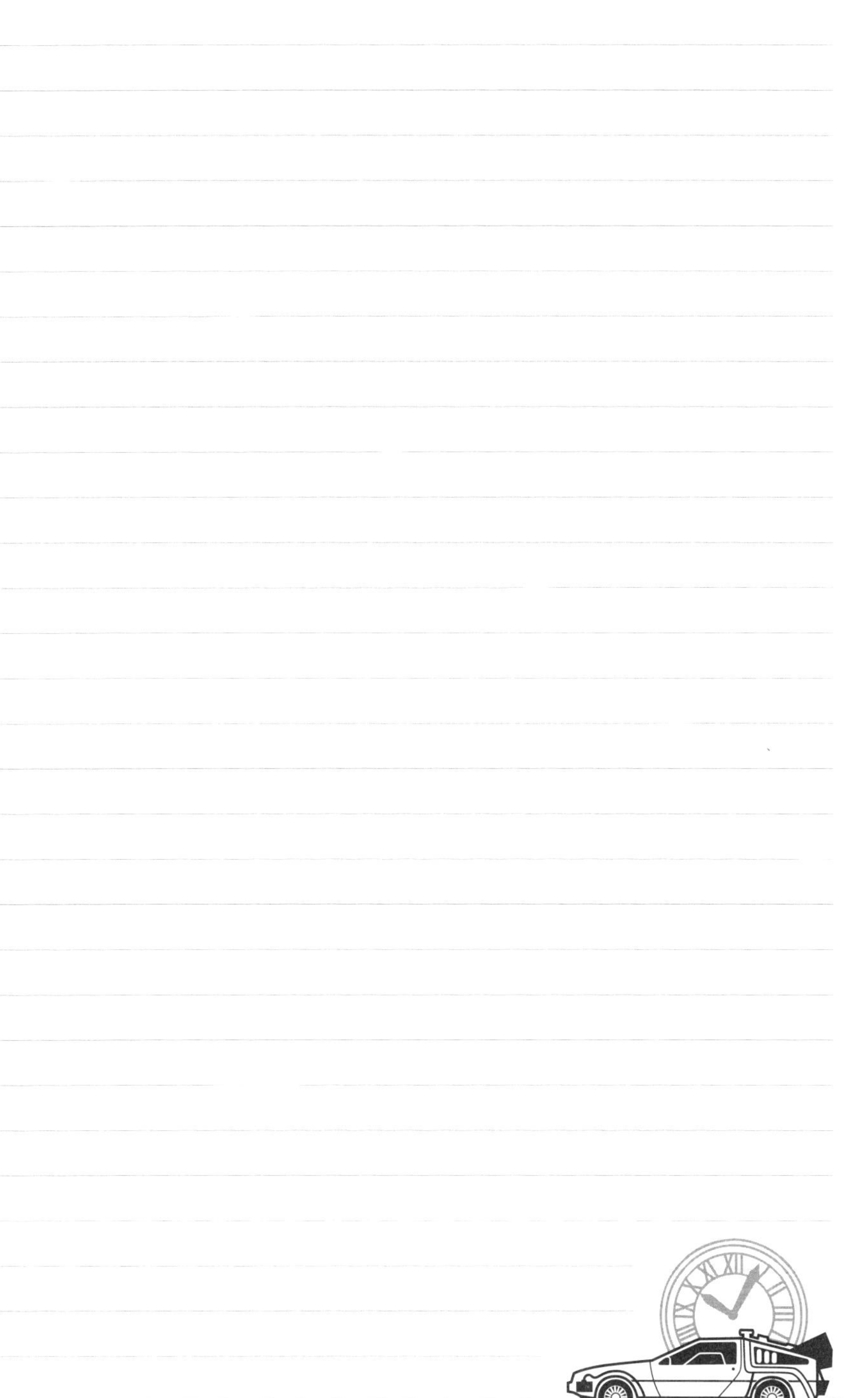

CALIFORNIA
OUTATIME

CALIFORNIA
OUTATIME

CALIFORNIA
OUTATIME

CALIFORNIA
OUTATIME

CALIFORNIA
OUTATIME

CALIFORNIA
OUTATIME

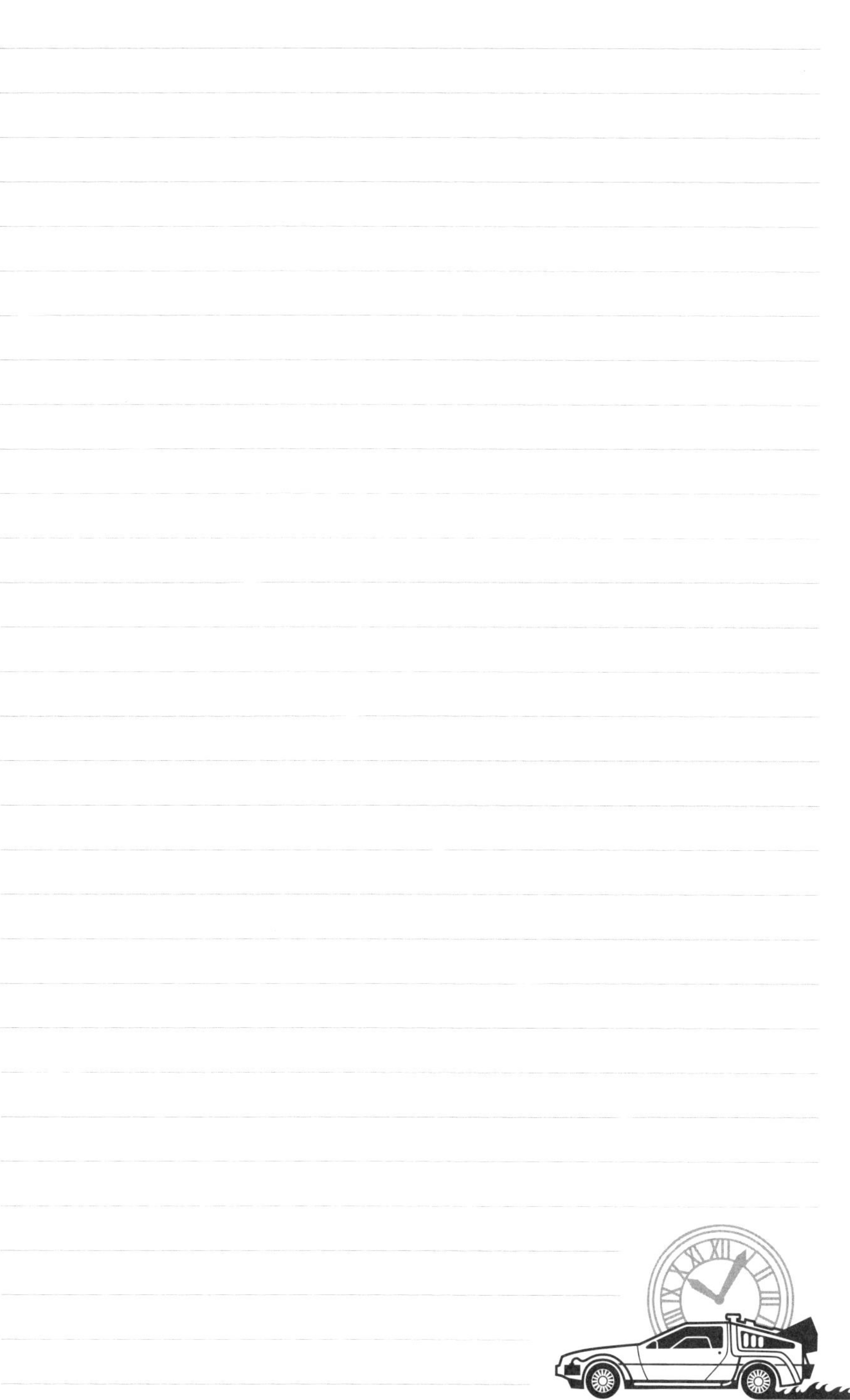

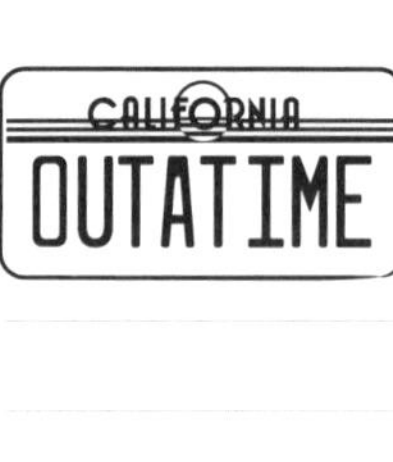
CALIFORNIA
OUTATIME

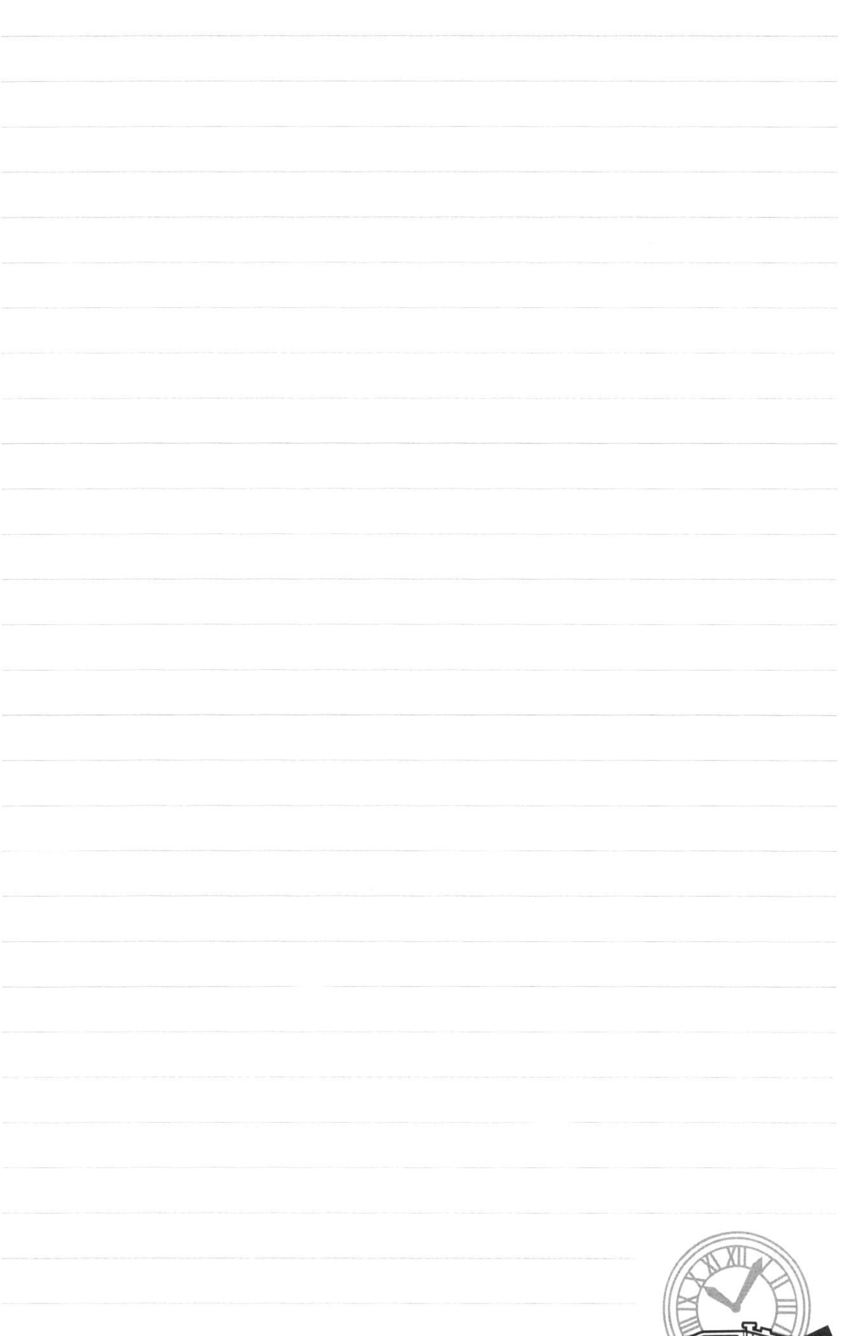

CALIFORNIA
OUTATIME

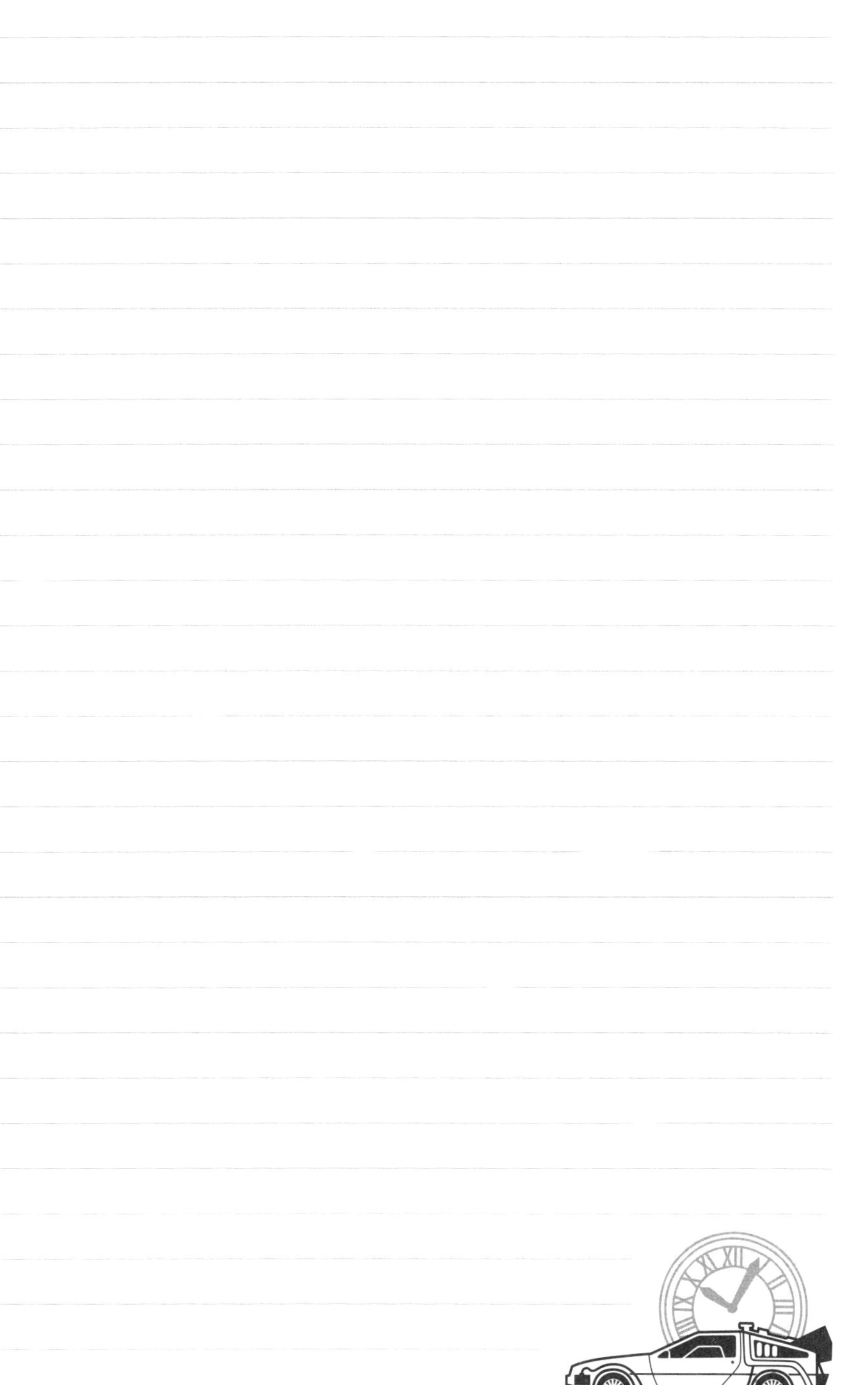

CALIFORNIA
OUTATIME

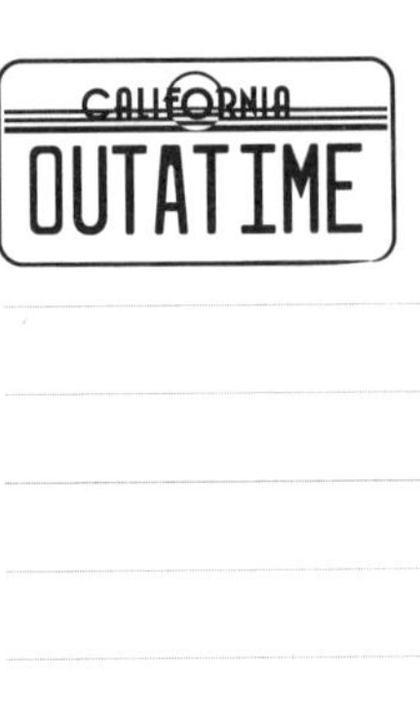
CALIFORNIA
OUTATIME

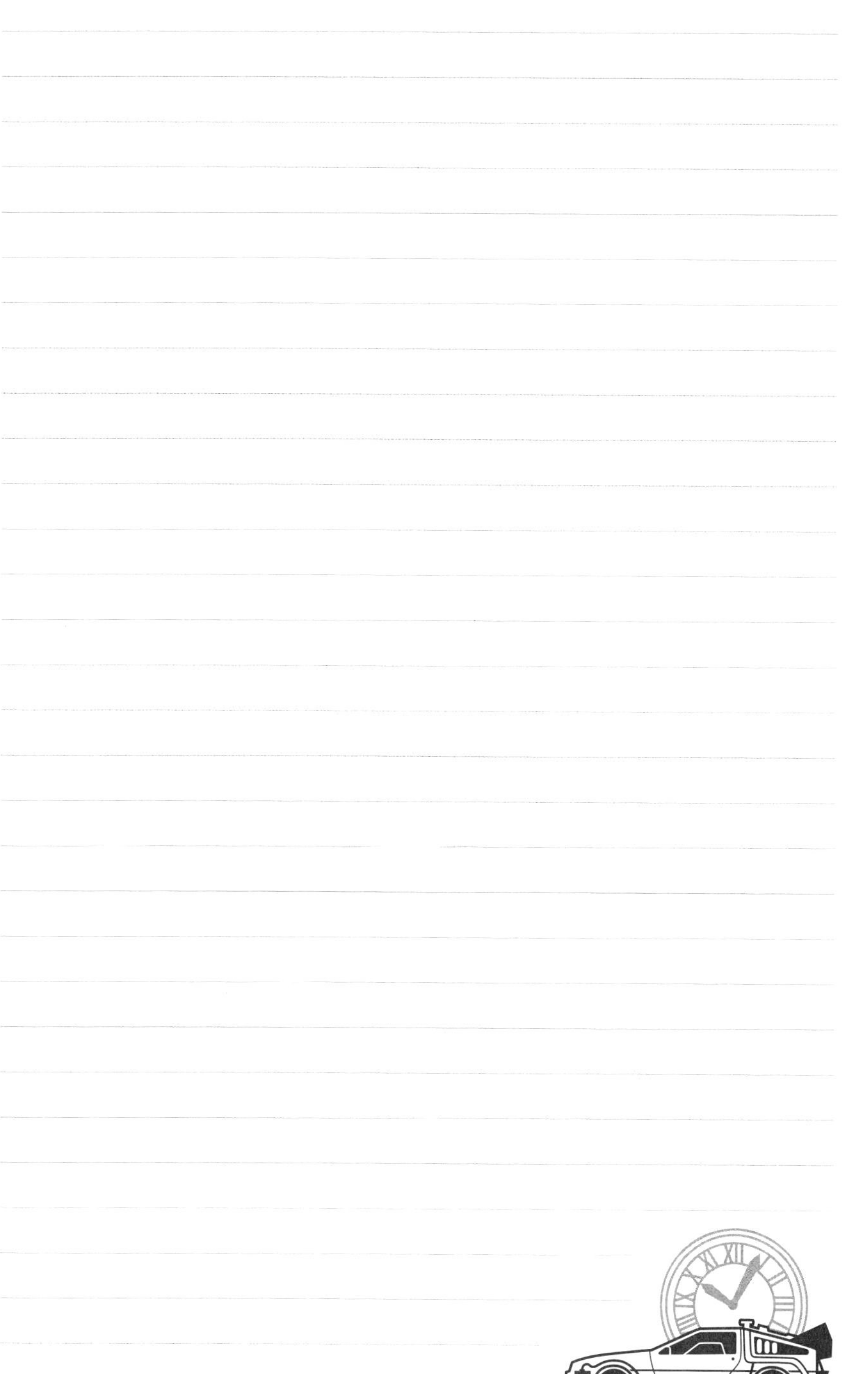

CALIFORNIA
OUTATIME

CALIFORNIA
OUTATIME

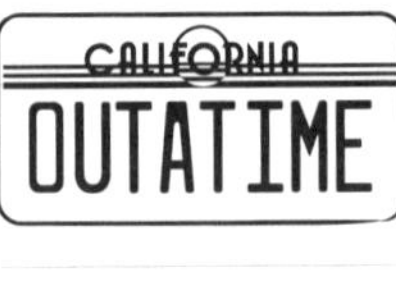
CALIFORNIA
OUTATIME

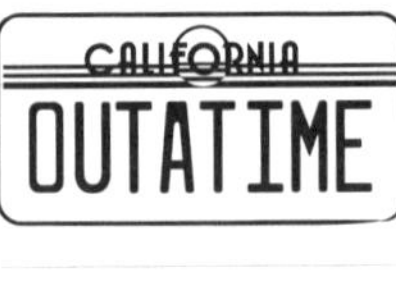
CALIFORNIA
OUTATIME

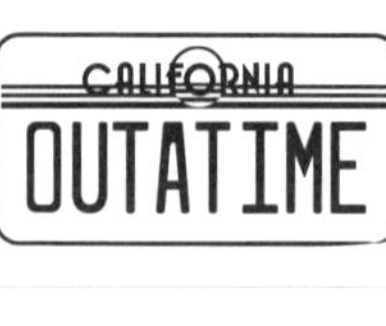
CALIFORNIA
OUTATIME

CALIFORNIA
OUTATIME

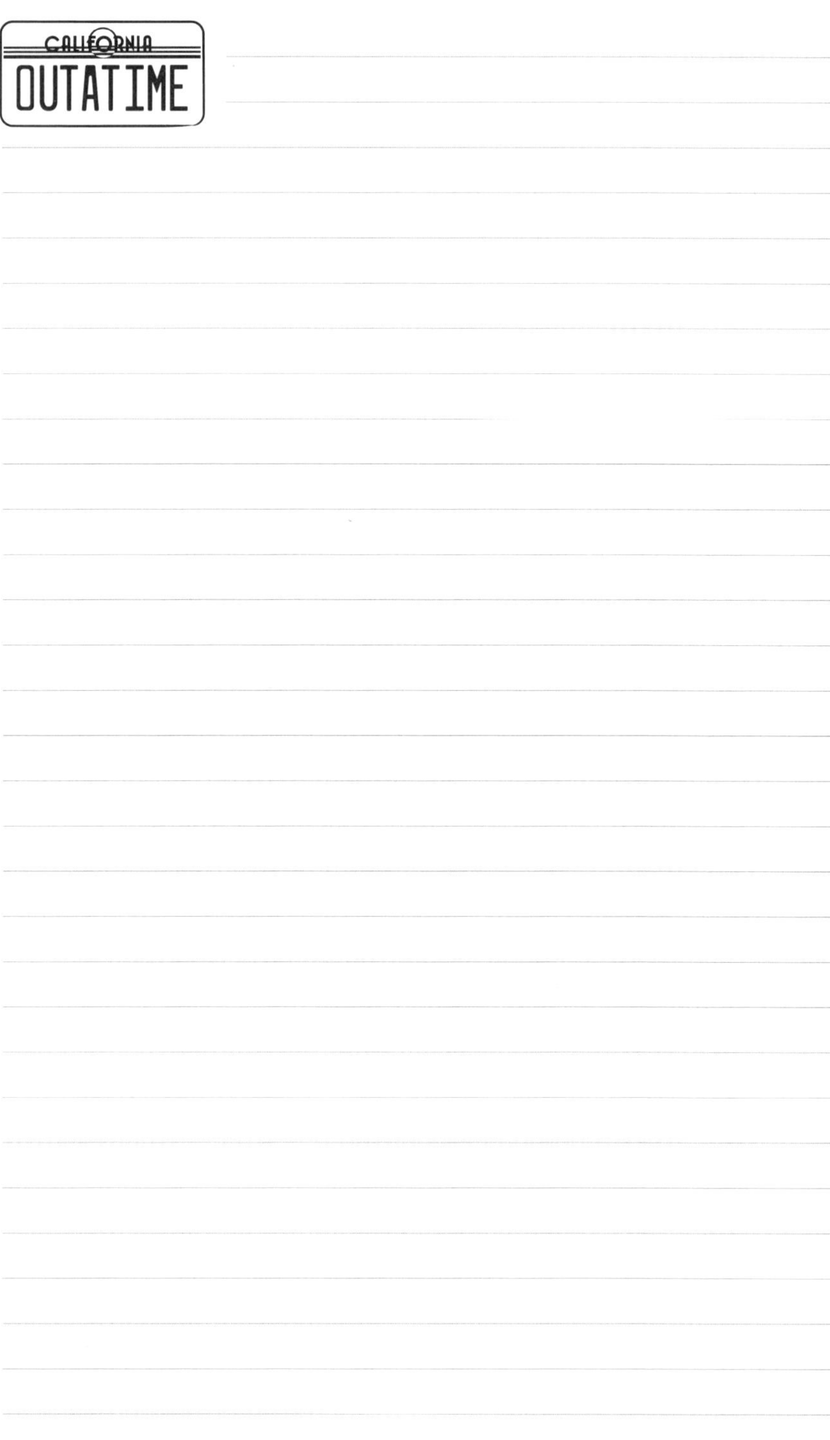
CALIFORNIA
OUTATIME

CALIFORNIA
OUTATIME

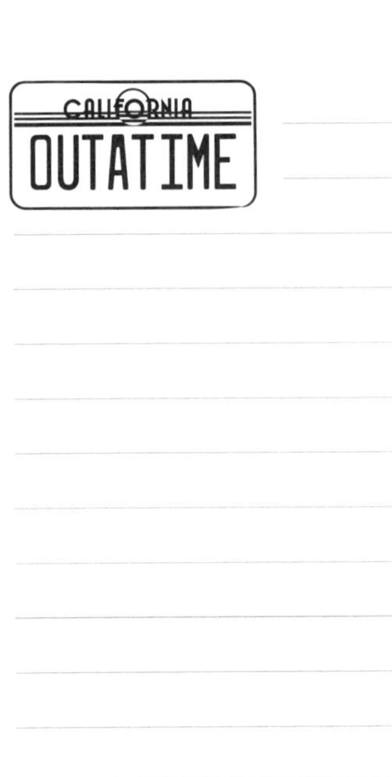
CALIFORNIA
OUTATIME

CALIFORNIA
OUTATIME

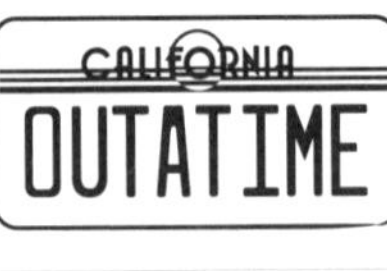
CALIFORNIA
OUTATIME

CALIFORNIA
OUTATIME

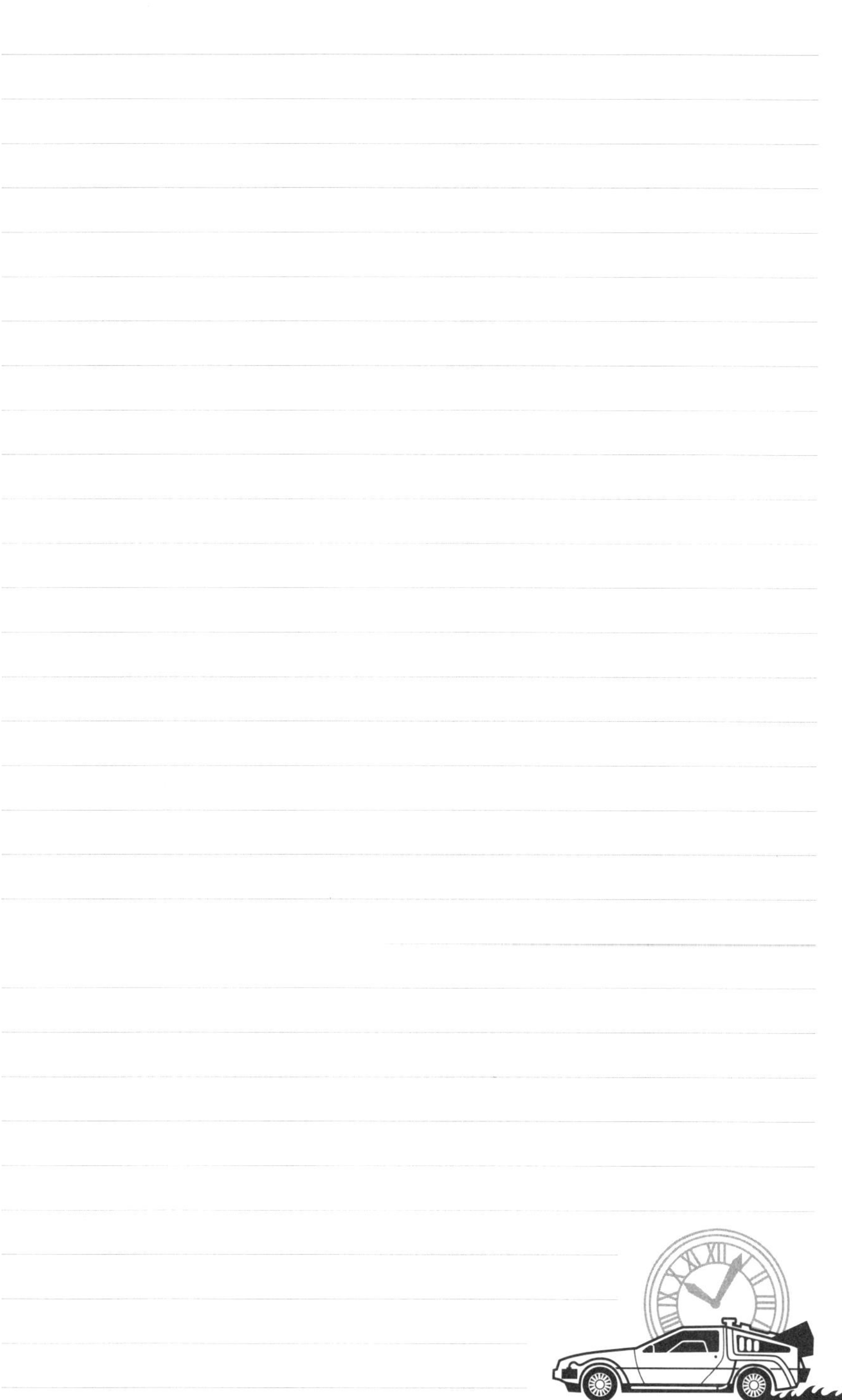

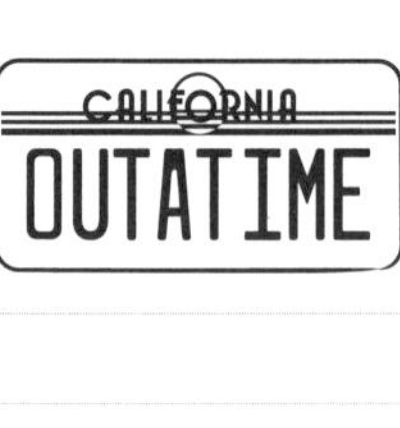
CALIFORNIA
OUTATIME

CALIFORNIA
OUTATIME

CALIFORNIA
OUTATIME

CALIFORNIA
OUTATIME

CALIFORNIA
OUTATIME

CALIFORNIA
OUTATIME

CALIFORNIA
OUTATIME

CALIFORNIA
OUTATIME

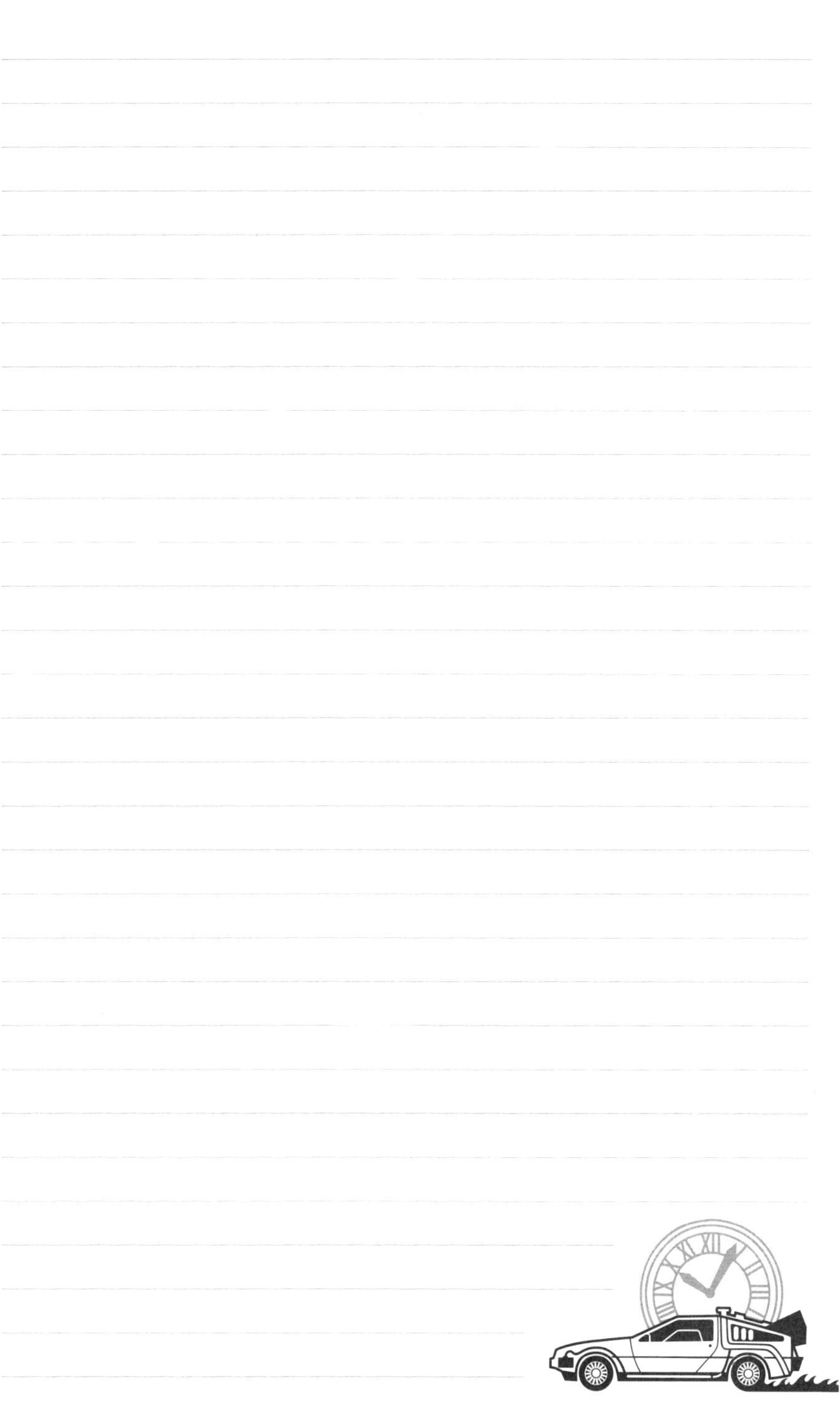

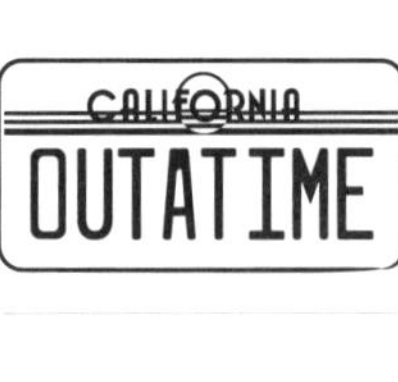
CALIFORNIA
OUTATIME

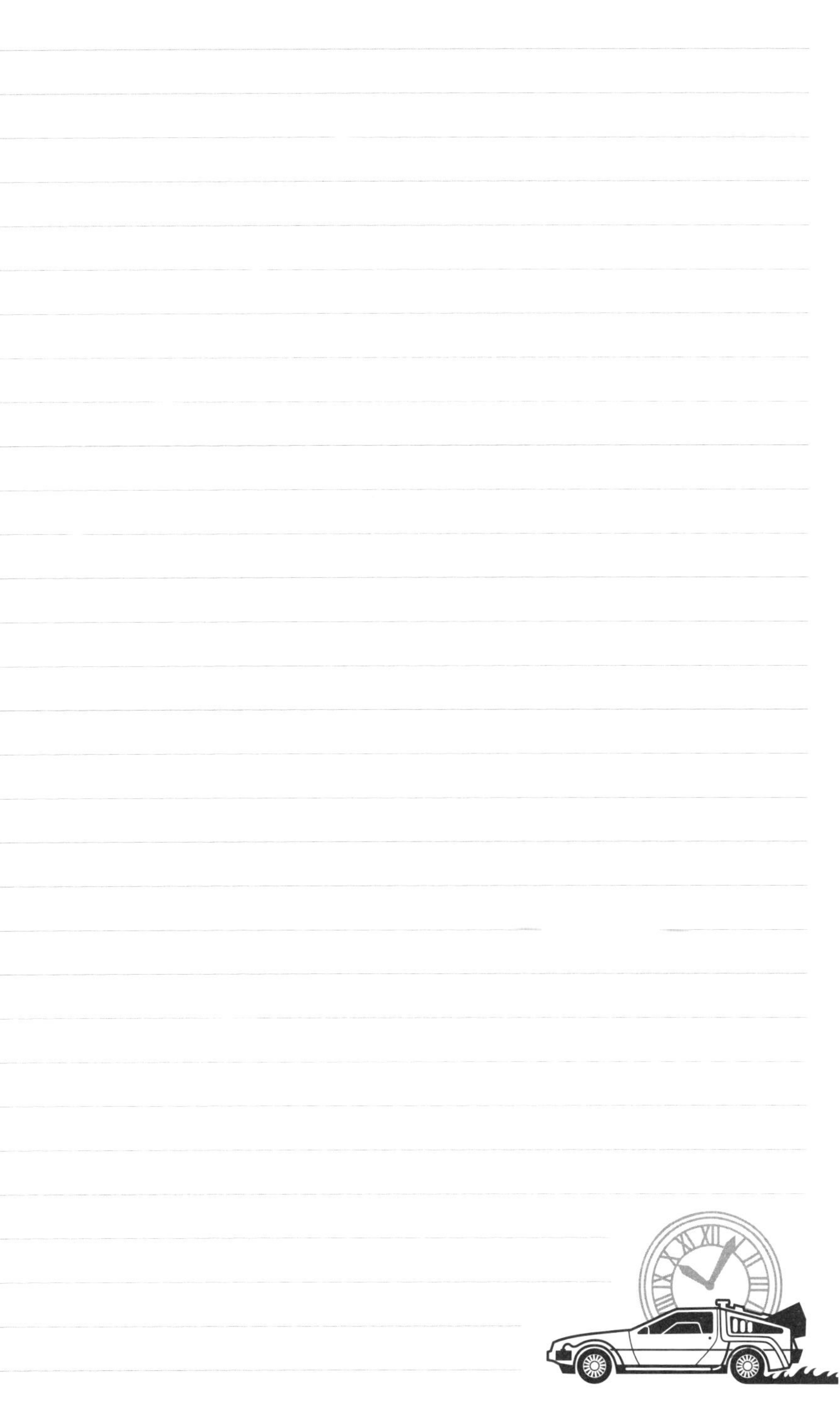

CALIFORNIA
OUTATIME

CALIFORNIA
OUTATIME

CALIFORNIA
OUTATIME

CALIFORNIA
OUTATIME

CALIFORNIA
OUTATIME

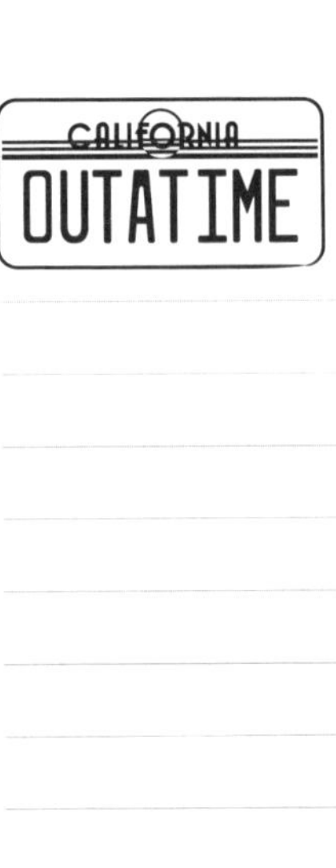
CALIFORNIA
OUTATIME

CALIFORNIA
OUTATIME

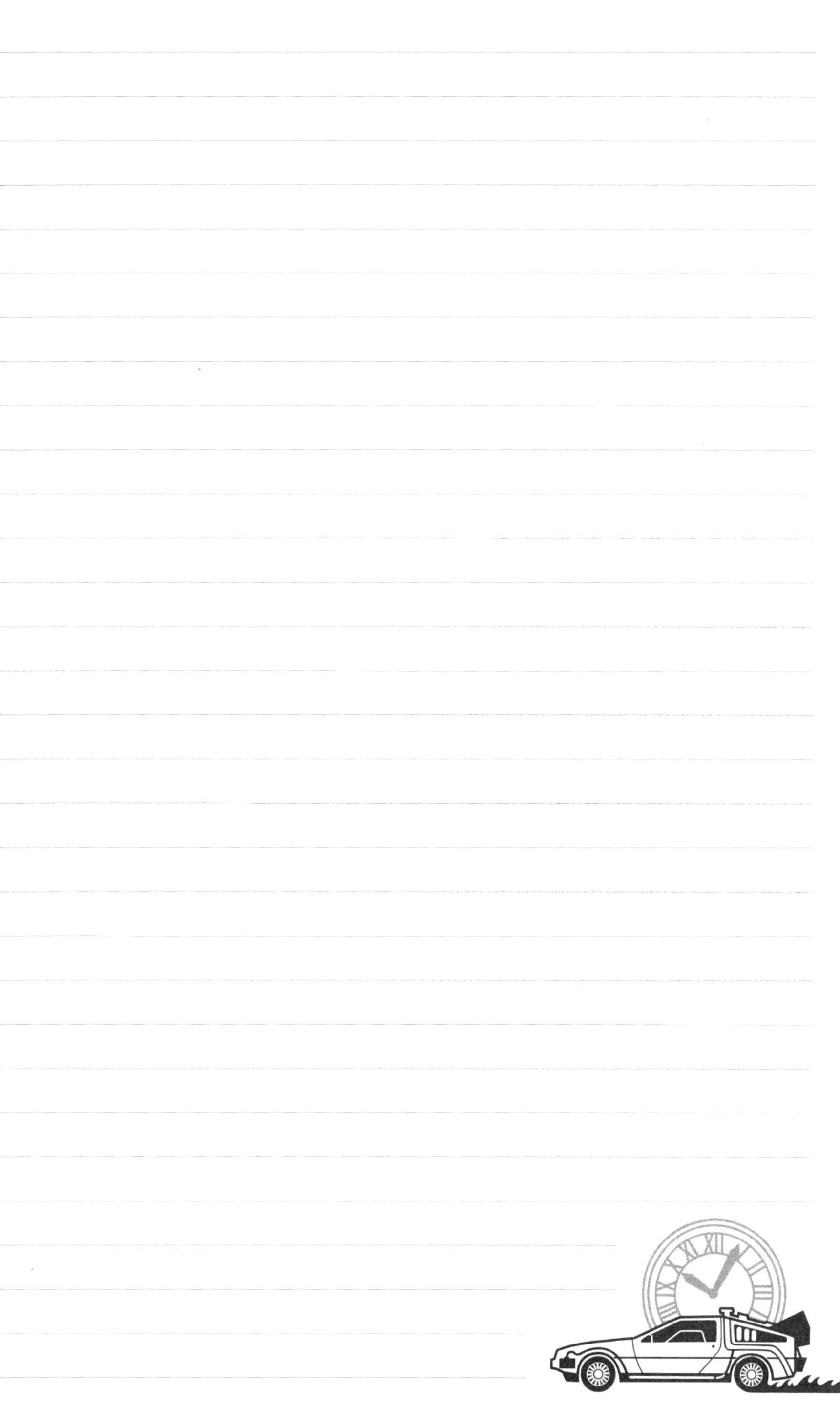

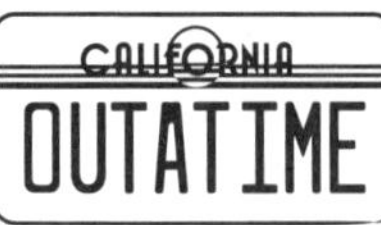
CALIFORNIA
OUTATIME

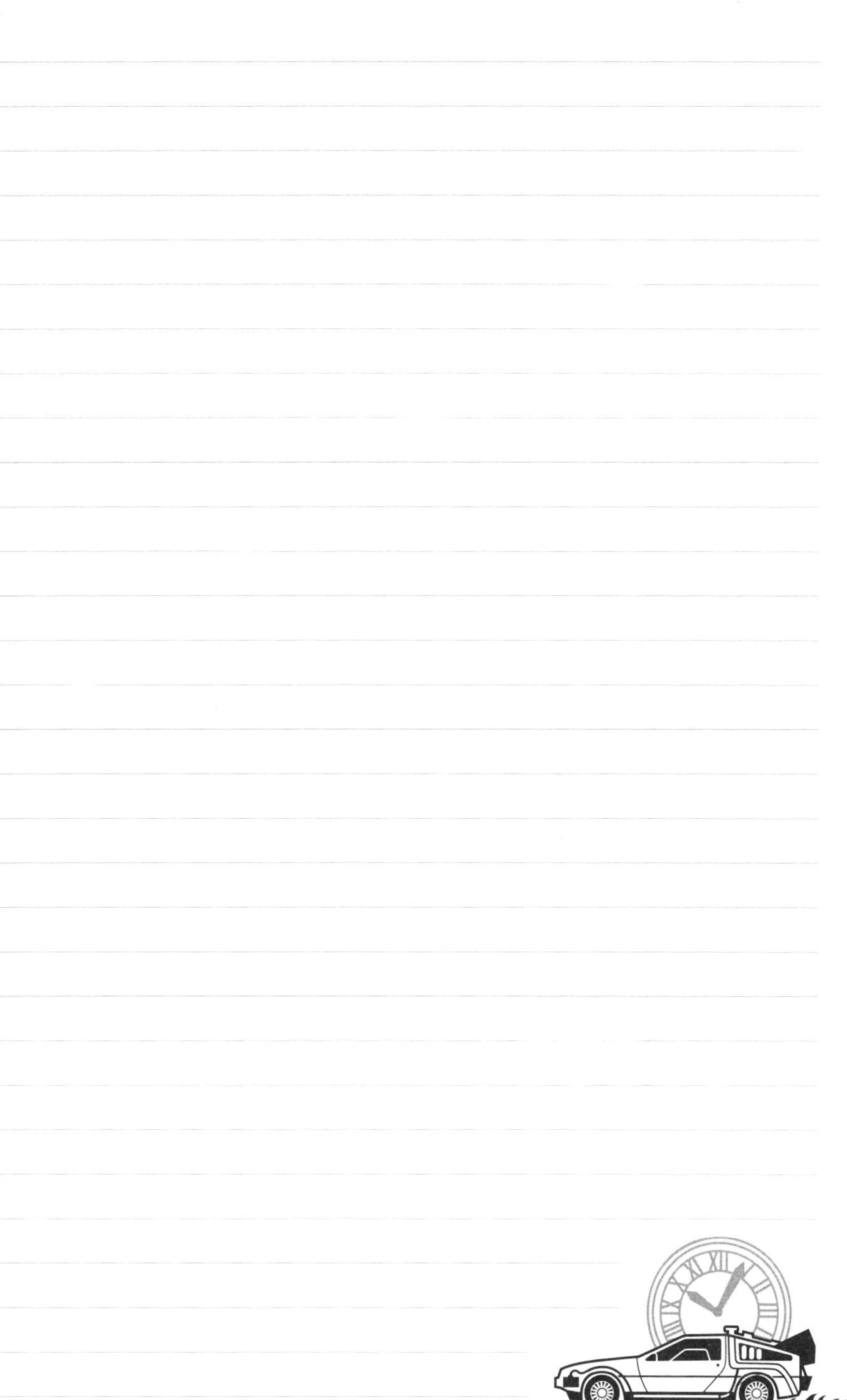

CALIFORNIA
OUTATIME

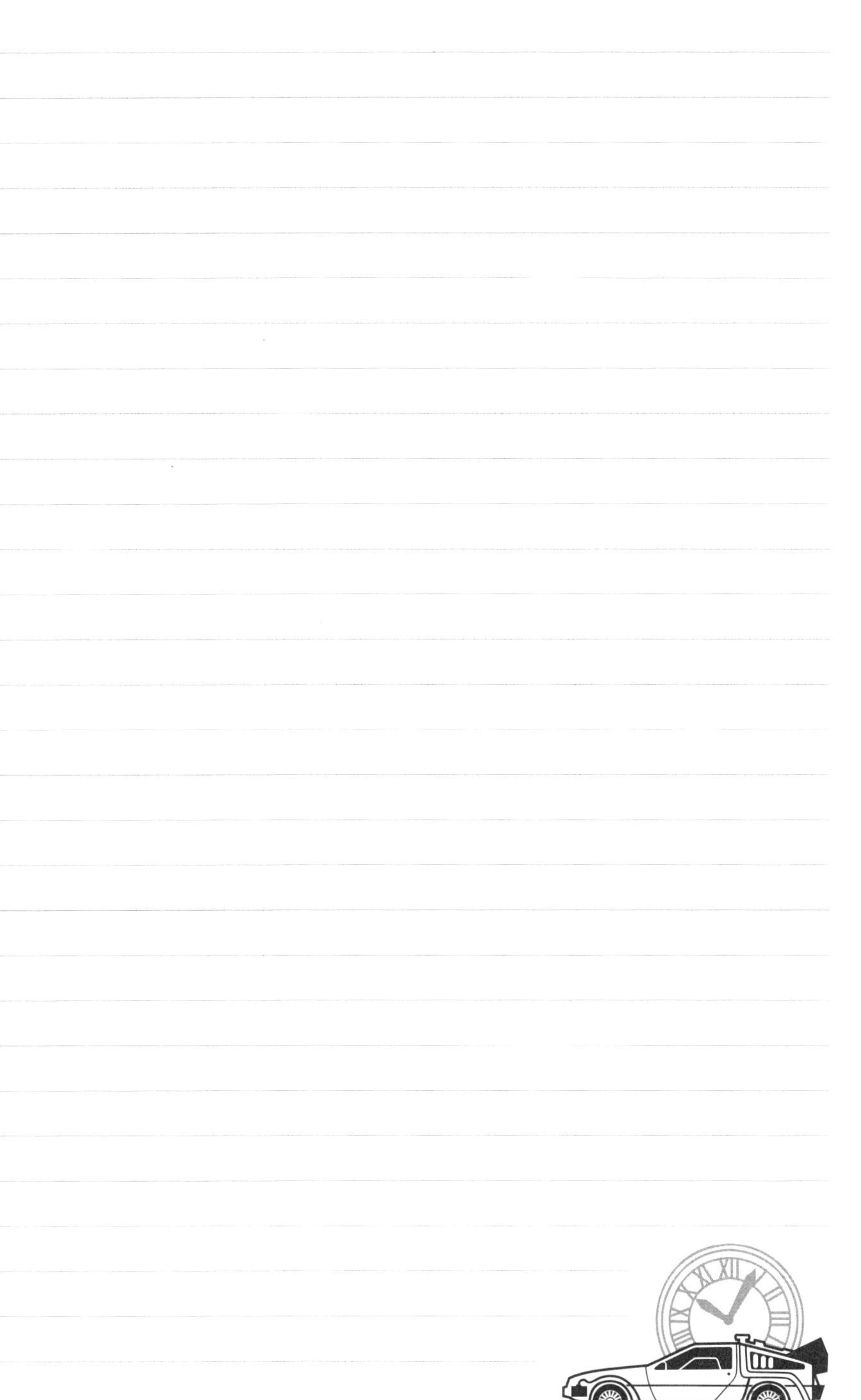

CALIFORNIA
OUTATIME

CALIFORNIA
OUTATIME

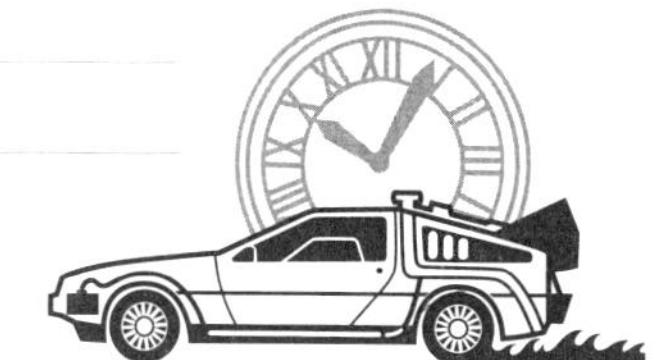

CALIFORNIA
OUTATIME

CALIFORNIA
OUTATIME

CALIFORNIA
OUTATIME

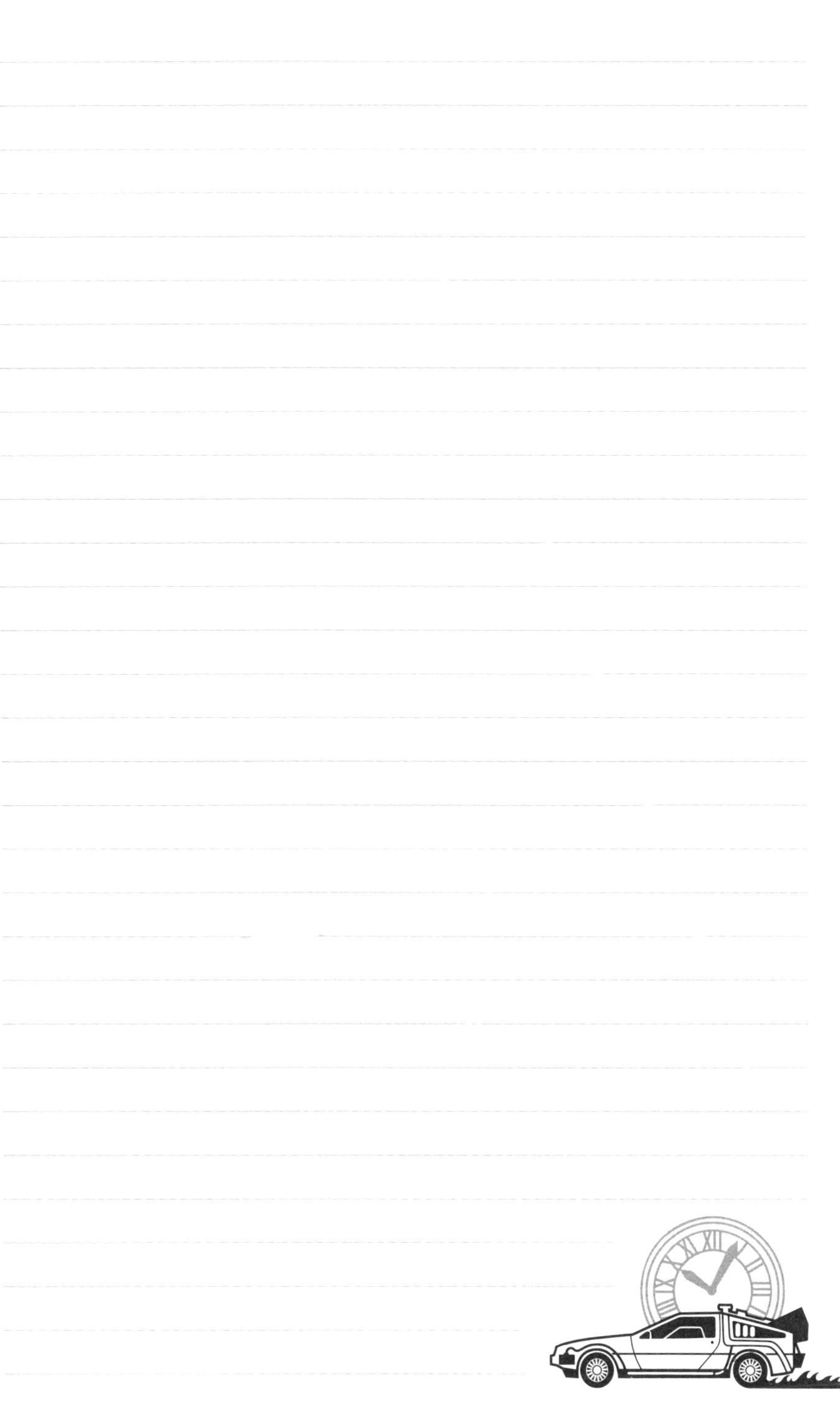

CALIFORNIA
OUTATIME

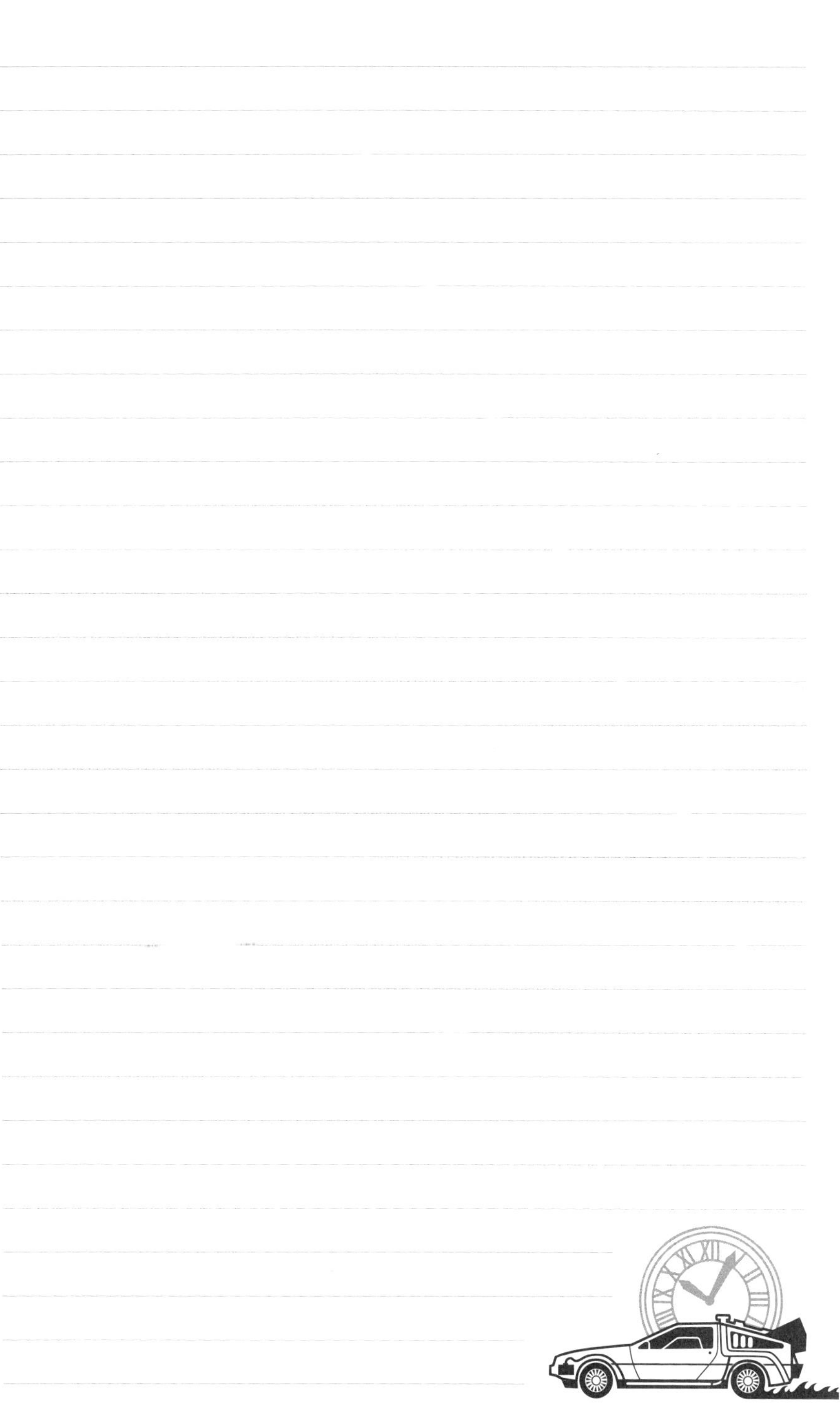

CALIFORNIA
OUTATIME

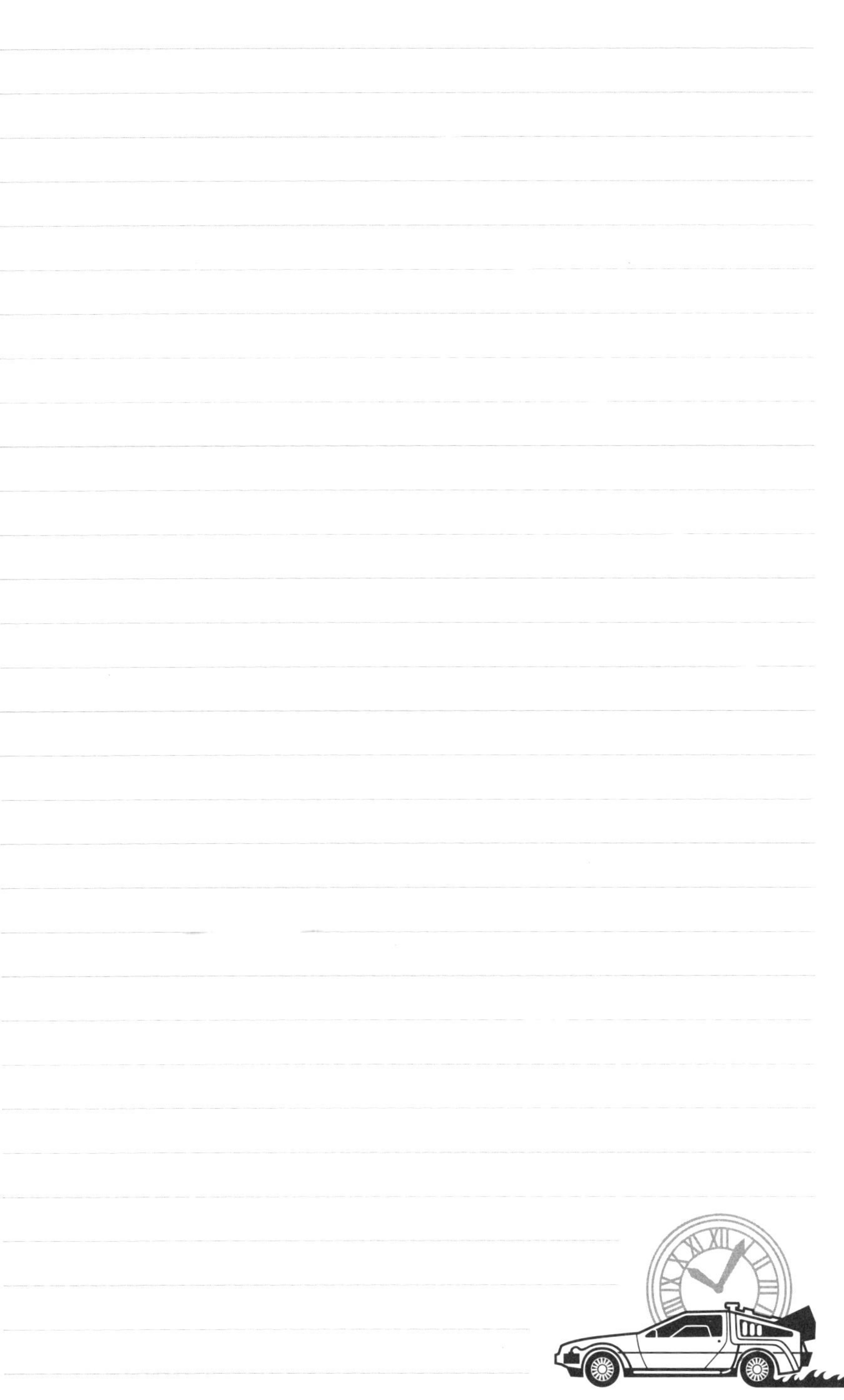

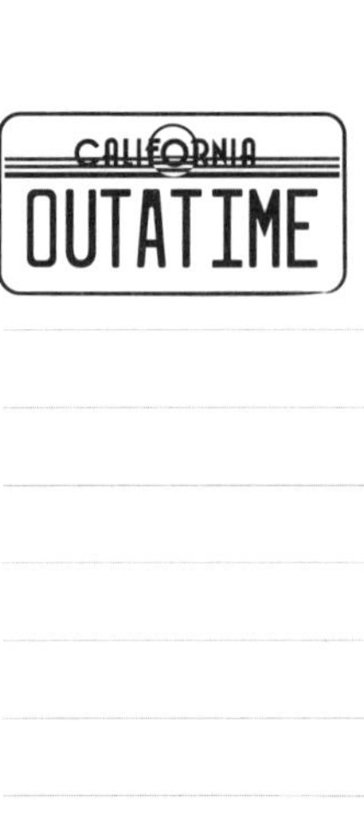
CALIFORNIA
OUTATIME

CALIFORNIA
OUTATIME

CALIFORNIA
OUTATIME

CALIFORNIA
OUTATIME

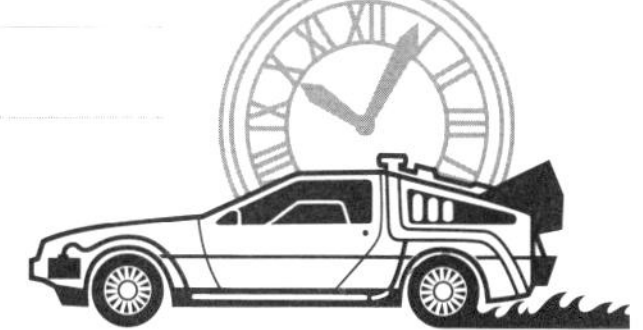

CALIFORNIA
OUTATIME

CALIFORNIA
OUTATIME

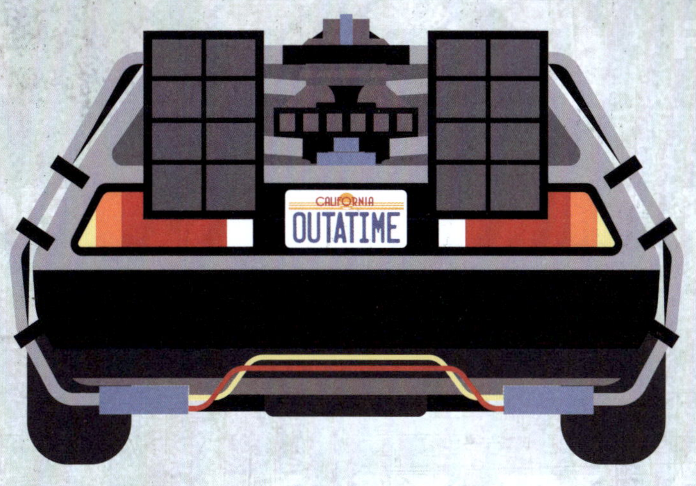

BACK TO THE FUTURE

INSIGHTS

www.insighteditions.com

MANUFACTURED IN CHINA

10 9 8 7 6 5 4 3 2 1

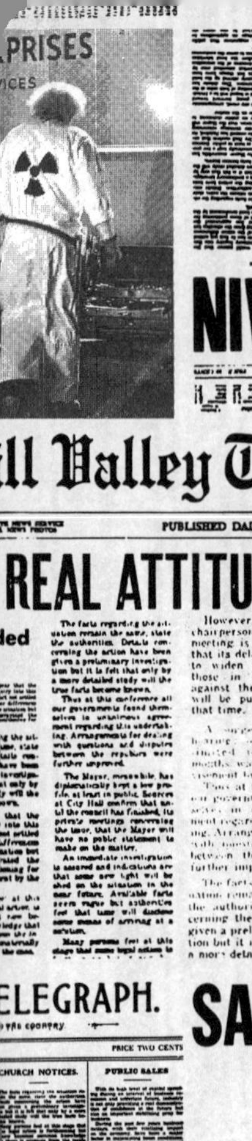

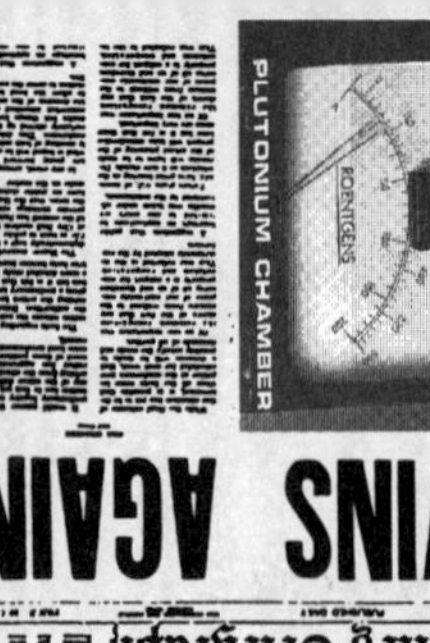

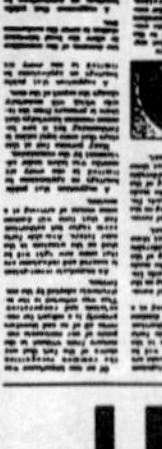

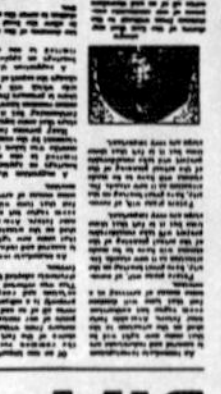

Hill Valley Telegraph

Hill Valley Man Wins Big At Races

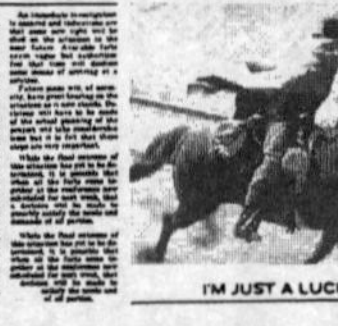

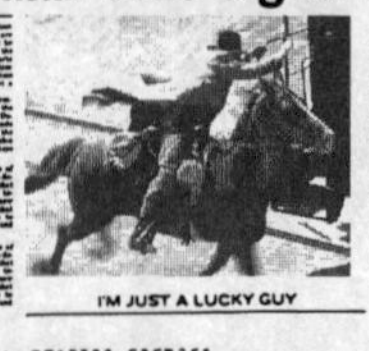

I'M JUST A LUCKY GUY

BIFF WINS AGAIN

Hill Valley Telegraph

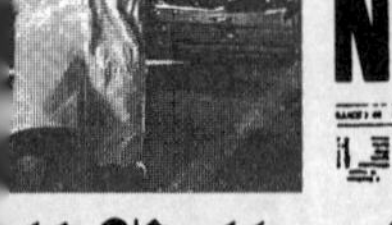

Hill Valley Telegraph

PUBLISHED DAILY — 10¢

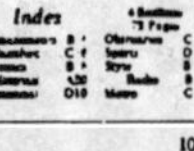

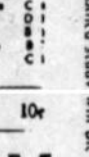

REAL ATTITUDE PROBLEM MCFLY

However, several committee chairpersons feel that the meeting is long overdue and that its delay has only served to widen the gap between those in favor and those against the resolutions that will be put before them at that time.

A suggestion that public hearings on applications be limited to one every six months was taken under advisement by the commission.

Thus at this conference all our governments found themselves in unanimous agreement regarding this undertaking. Arrangements for dealing with questions and disputes between the republics were further improved.

The facts regarding the situation remain the same, state the authorities. Details concerning the action have been given a preliminary investigation but it is felt that only by a more detailed study will the

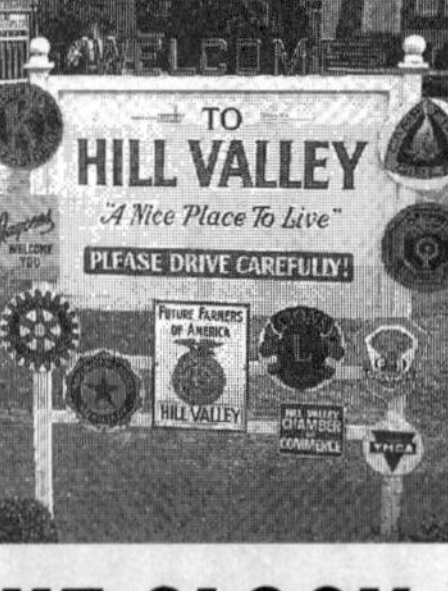

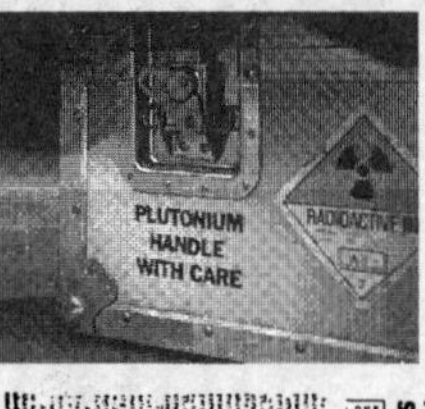

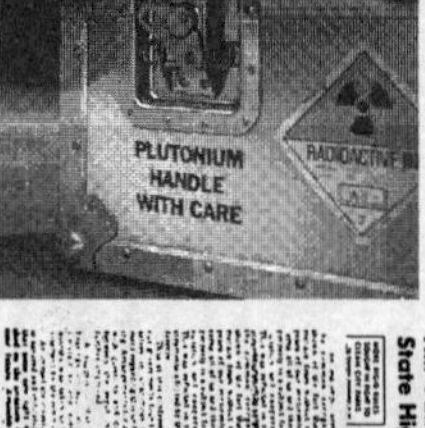

I SENT HIM INTO THE FUTURE

Hill Valley to get Added State Highway Funds

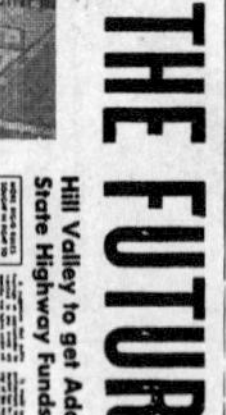

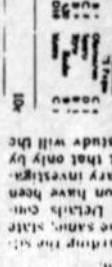

TELEGRAPH.

PRICE TWO CENTS

CHURCH NOTICES.

PUBLIC SALES

CHIEFTAIN STOMACH BITTERS

Leaders Meet To Plan

Our New LOCATION at 226 Center Street

EMERSON'S General MERCANTILE CO.

SAVE THE CLOCK TOWER

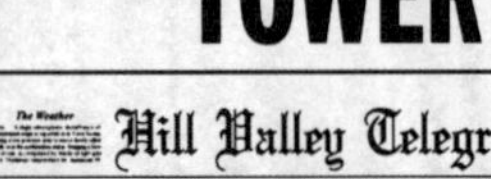

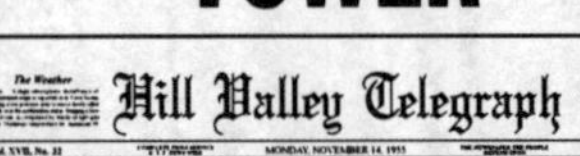

Hill Valley Telegraph

MONDAY, NOVEMBER 14, 1955

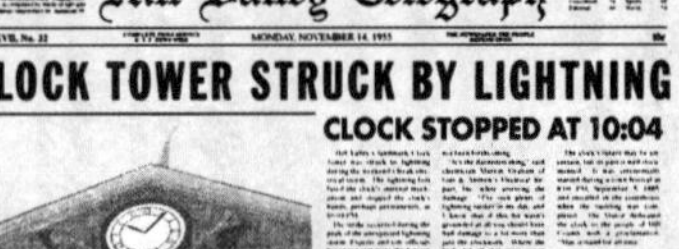

CLOCK TOWER STRUCK BY LIGHTNING

CLOCK STOPPED AT 10:04

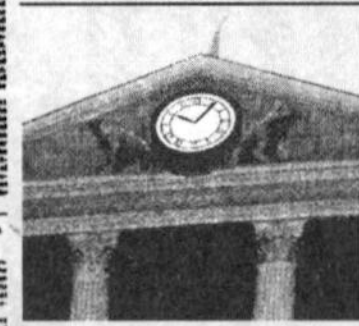

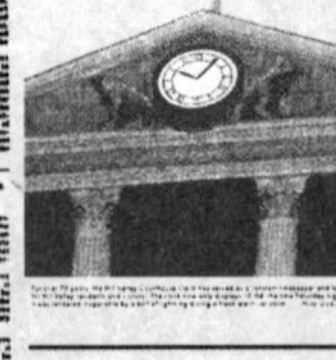

Plans To Launch Tests of New Toll System Here

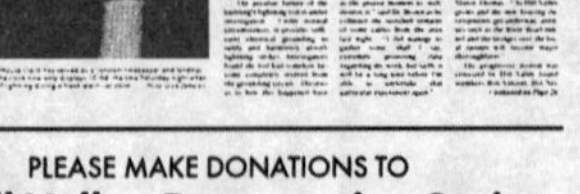

PLEASE MAKE DONATIONS TO

The Hill Valley Preservation Society

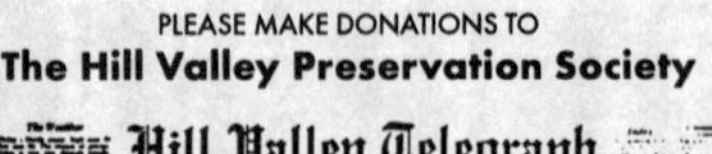

Hill Valley Telegraph

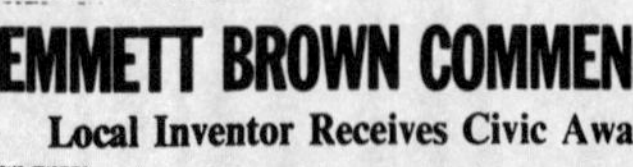

EMMETT BROWN COMMENDED

Local Inventor Receives Civic Award

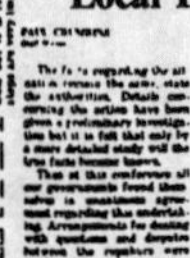

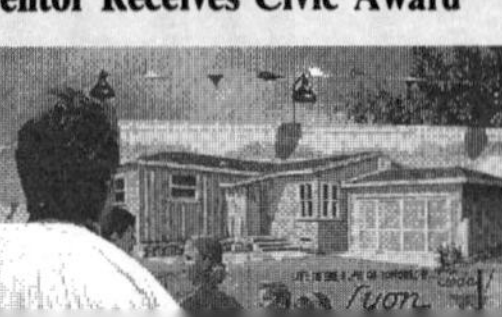

HILL VALLEY TELEGRAPH

BROWN MANSION DESTROYED

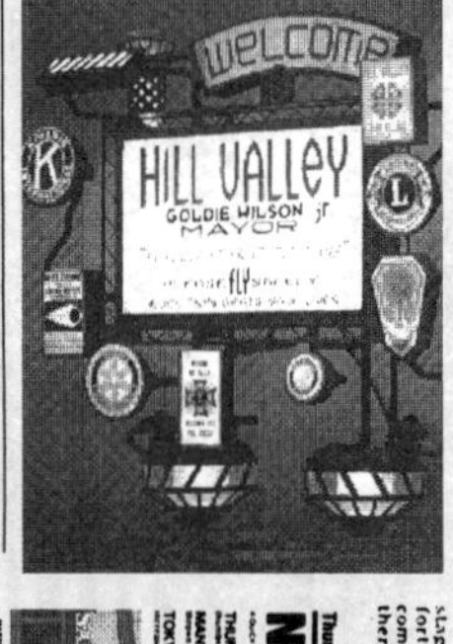

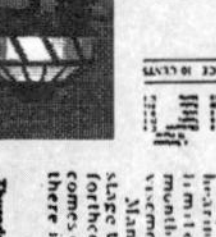

NEWSLINE

Thursday, OCTOBER 22, 2015

THUMB BANDITS STRIKE

MAN KILLED BY FALLING LITTER

TOKYO STOCKS UP

SHREDDING FOR CHARITY

PRESIDENT SHREDDED, SAYS

JAWS WITHOUT BITE

KELP PRICE INCREASE

PITCHER SUSPENDED FOR BIONIC ARM USE

SLAMBALL PLAYOFFS BEGIN

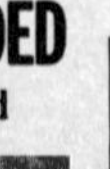

GANG JA...

Hoverboard Rampage Dest...

Gang Leader had Bionic Overloads

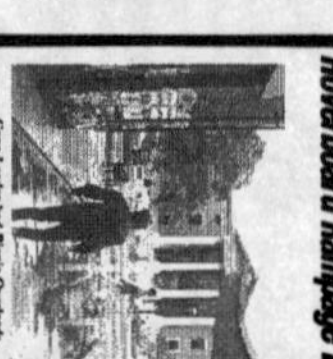

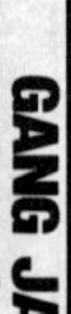

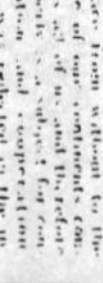

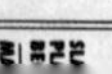